T0300661

Best Easy Day Hikes
Acadia National Park

Help Us Keep This Guide Up to Date

Every effort has been made by the authors and editors to make this guide as accurate and useful as possible. However, many things can change after a guide is published—regulations change, facilities come under new management, and so forth.

We would love to hear from you concerning your experience with this guide and how you feel it could be improved and kept up to date. While we may not be able to respond to all comments and suggestions, we'll take them to heart, and we'll also make certain to share them with the authors. Please send your comments and suggestions to 64 South Main Street, Essex, CT 06426.

Thanks for your input!

Best Easy Day Hikes Series

Best Easy Day Hikes
Acadia
National Park

Fifth Edition

Dolores Kong and Dan Ring

FALCONGUIDES

ESSEX, CONNECTICUT

FALCONGUIDES®

An imprint of The Globe Pequot Publishing Group, Inc.
64 South Main Street
Essex, CT 06426
www.globepequot.com

Falcon and FalconGuides are registered trademarks and Make Adventure Your Story is a trademark of Globe Pequot Publishing Group, Inc.

Distributed by NATIONAL BOOK NETWORK

British Library Cataloguing in Publication Information available

Library of Congress Cataloging-in-Publication Data

Names: Kong, Dolores, author. | Ring, Dan (Daniel), author.
Title: Best easy day hikes Acadia National Park / Dolores Kong and Dan Ring.
Description: Fifth edition. | Essex, Connecticut : FalconGuides : Distributed by
    National Book Network, [2025] | Series: Best easy day hikes series | Fourth
    edition published in 2019. | Summary: "The authors provide details on day
    hikes in Maine's Acadia National Park, the first national park east of the
    Mississippi and one of the most popular destinations in the park system" —
    Provided by publisher.
Identifiers: LCCN 2024038696 (print) | LCCN 2024038697 (ebook) | ISBN
    9781493079612 (paper ; acid-free paper) | ISBN 9781493079629 (epub)
Subjects: LCSH: Day hiking—Maine—Acadia National Park—Guidebooks. |
    Hiking—Maine—Acadia National Park—Guidebooks. | Walking—Maine—Aca-
    dia National Park—Guidebooks. | Backpacking—Maine—Acadia National
    Park—Guidebooks. | Trails—Maine—Acadia National Park—Guidebooks. |
    Acadia National Park (Me.)—Description and travel. | Acadia National Park
    (Me.)—Guidebooks.
Classification: LCC GV199.42.M22 A323 2025 (print) | LCC GV199.42.M22
    (ebook) | DDC 796.5109741—dc23/eng/20241223
LC record available at https://lccn.loc.gov/2024038696
LC ebook record available at https://lccn.loc.gov/2024038697

♾ ™ The paper used in this publication meets the minimum requirements of
American National Standard for Information Sciences—Permanence of Paper for
Printed Library Materials, ANSI/NISO Z39.48-1992.

Contents

The Hikes

Mount Desert Island West of Somes Sound 9

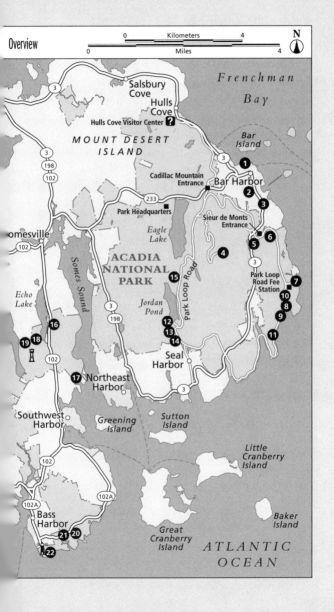

Kilometers   0   4

Miles   0   4

N

Frenchman
Bay

Salsbury
Cove
Hulls
Cove

Hulls Cove Visitor Center ?

MOUNT DESERT
ISLAND

Bar
Island

Cadillac Mountain
Entrance

Bar Harbor

Park Headquarters

Sieur de Monts
Entrance

Eagle
Lake

ACADIA
NATIONAL
PARK

Park Loop Road Fee
Station

Echo
Lake

Somes Sound

Jordan
Pond

omesville

Seal
Harbor

Northeast
Harbor

Southwest
Harbor

Greening
Island

Sutton
Island

Little
Cranberry
Island

Bass
Harbor

Great
Cranberry
Island

Baker
Island

ATLANTIC
OCEAN

Acknowledgments

For sharing their knowledge and passion for Acadia Nation: Park, and for being so generous with their time, we'd lik to thank Wanda Moran, Charlie Jacobi, Gary Stellpflug David Schlag, Christian Barter, Jeff Chapin, Bruce Cor nery, Lynne Dominy, Vincent Sproul, John Kelly, Amand Pollock, Kevin Schneider, Christie Anastasia, David Mansk Kathy Grant, Stuart West, Karen Anderson, Anne Warne and the rest of the Acadia National Park staff, past and pre ent; Margaret Coffin Brown of the National Park Servic Jill Weber; Marla S. O'Byrne; Maureen and Gerry Fournie Michael Good; Susan Hayward; Tim Henderson; Jim Li nane; Jack Russell; Eastern National; and the Friends Acadia.

And we'd like to thank family and friends who' already hiked the trails of Acadia with us or who one d will: April, Thomas, Sharon, Michelle, Judy, Stacey, Be Jen, Phil, Sebastian, Miranda, Laura, Mike, Jenna, Winsto and too many others to name.

Introduction

Maine's Acadia National Park is a place like no other.

You can stroll along Ocean Path and be awestruck by the contrast of pink-granite cliffs, blue skies, and white surf. From atop Cadillac, the highest mountain on the US Atlantic Seaboard, you can see fog rolling in over Frenchman Bay below, even as the sun shines brightly above. And over on the shores of Jordan Pond, you can take part in one of the most civilized of afternoon rituals, tea and popovers, with the distinct mountains known as the Bubbles as nature's backdrop.

No wonder artists, millionaires, generations of families, and even presidents—notably Barack Obama in 2010—have been attracted to all that's preserved in Acadia.

In fact, the place means so much to area residents and visitors that in 1919 Acadia became the first national park created east of the Mississippi that remains a national park, after starting as a national monument in 1916. It is also the first national park to consist primarily of privately donated lands and the first to have trail maintenance funded by an endowment, Acadia Trails Forever, coming from $4 million in park user fees and federal appropriations and $9 million in private donations from Friends of Acadia, a private nonprofit organization based in Bar Harbor.

Over the years the scenery here has inspired such passion that nineteenth-century painters Thomas Cole and Frederic Church, of the Hudson River School, came here to capture the landscape; one of the wealthiest men in America, John D. Rockefeller Jr., donated millions and left miles of picturesque carriage roads and uniquely designed stone bridges; and prime mover George B. Dorr dedicated his life and exhausted his family fortune to create the park.

The scenery at Acadia even drew President Barack Obama and his family in July 2010 to the views from the top of Cadillac and along the Ship Harbor and Bass Harbor Head Light Trails.

Acadia's hiking trails won more national recognition in 2022 when they were added to the National Register of Historic Places, establishing the largest hiking trails system on the federal list of places worth preserving. Placed on the register as "The Mount Desert Island Hiking Trail System," the Acadia National Park network consists of 109 maintained trails and paths covering about 117 miles.

Today nearly 4 million visits a year make Acadia one of the top-ten most visited and popular national parks, even though it's among the smallest in land area.

Acadia is so attractive that visitation since 2013 jumped by 72 percent to 3.87 million visits in 2023. The increases in visits prompted the National Park Service to launch a major effort to approve new ways to deal with frequent overcrowding and increasing traffic at the park during peak season.

In 2021, the park started a vehicle reservation system for Cadillac Mountain, the number-one attraction in Acadia. The reservation system has eliminated unsafe traffic and parking congestion that had occurred on the summit in prior years, according to the NPS.

Vehicle reservations, in addition to an entrance pass, are now required for the Cadillac Summit Road from the Wednesday before Memorial Day to late October. Vehicle reservations can be obtained online at recreation.gov for a minimal fee.

Since the last edition of this book was published in 2016, parking is now even tighter at many trailheads and popular destinations such as Jordan Pond and Sand Beach during the busy months, underscoring the importance for visitors to use the fare-free Island Explorer shuttle system.

But with about 155 miles of hiking trails and 45 miles of carriage roads throughout its nearly 50,000 acres (including almost 13,000 acres under conservation easement), the park still provides plenty of opportunities for tranquility as well as experiencing nature, history, geology, and culture.

This guide is for those with limited time to hike Acadia, or for those who want to sample only the easiest or most popular trails. This fifth edition of *Best Easy Day Hikes Acadia National Park* was researched as part of an update of our more comprehensive guide, *Hiking Acadia National Park*.

Many of the trails described here are very easy and suitable for families with young children, but some are more challenging hikes that are among the most popular in the area, bringing you to grand mountaintop vistas. The "Trail Finder" section of this guide offers a listing of hikes by characteristic, such as "Best Hikes for Children" or "Best Hikes for Great Views."

Excluded from this guide are cliff climbs and Isle au Haut and Schoodic Peninsula trails, which are in the more comprehensive *Hiking Acadia National Park*. Also excluded: the 45 miles of carriage roads that are shared with bicyclists, horseback riders, and horse-drawn carriages.

Since the first edition of this guide, new trails have been added and trail names have been changed to reflect a comprehensive multiyear, multimillion-dollar effort by the NPS and Acadia Trails Forever to update the historic network. The extensive system includes Native American paths, old roads, and trails built by local village improvement associations near the turn of the twentieth century, as documented by the NPS's Olmsted Center for Landscape Preservation.

For example, what was called the Bear Brook Trail in the first edition is now the Champlain North Ridge Trail, as already reflected on trailhead signs.

But a note of caution: In some cases the NPS may not yet have updated trail signs—it's a multiyear process—even though the plan is to ultimately rename some of the historic trails.

This fifth edition provides details on Island Explorer bus stops near trailheads. If you visit during peak season (summer through fall foliage season), you can take advantage of th increasingly popular, fare-free, and eco-friendly way of getting around Acadia. The bus driver may also make specially requested stops, if it's safe to do so. Be sure to buy a par pass to help support the Island Explorer and other program offered by the NPS.

Aside from hiking some of the trails described here, visito may also want to stop at the Abbe Museum, the Wild Garde of Acadia, and the Nature Center, all located at the Sieur Monts entrance to the park, on ME 3 south of Bar Harbor.

The Abbe Museum, founded by Dr. Robert Abbe, a pi neer of the medical use of radium, celebrates and preserv the culture and heritage of Native Americans who lived he thousands of years before European emigrants set eyes on t Maine coast. In addition to the seasonal museum at the Sie de Monts entrance, there is a year-round museum facility downtown Bar Harbor.

The Wild Gardens of Acadia and the Nature Cent introduce the visitor to some of the flora and fauna Acadia. The whole Sieur de Monts Spring area, especia the gardens in early morning, is an excellent bird-watchi spot, with the possibility of sighting warblers, woodpecke flycatchers, and thrushes.

Weather

In the space of an hour or less, the weather in Aca can change from sunny and warm to wind-whipped ra especially on mountaintops. Summer highs average 70°F to 90°F, although fog can be common, with lows in the 50s. In the spring, highs average 50°F to 60°F, and it can be rainy. The fall brings highs in the low 70s, but rain or snow can be expected. In the winter, temperatures range from below zero to 30°F, and snowfall averages about 60 inches a year. Be prepared, no matter what season you are hiking.

Climate change is a big issue at the park, leading to such effects as a longer busy season that strains park staff, as well as more powerful rainstorms. In early January 2024, twin rainstorms damaged roads, uprooted trees, and eroded the coastline and hiking trails. And a rainstorm in June 2021 damaged some hiking trails and required the temporary closure and repair of 10 miles of historic carriage roads.

Rules and Regulations

Pets must be kept on a leash no longer than 6 feet and are not allowed on ladder trails or in public water supplies. They are also prohibited on Sand Beach from June 15 up until the weekend after Labor Day and Echo Lake from May 15 to September 15; public buildings; ranger-led programs; and the Wild Gardens of Acadia. (Service animals are an exception to these rules.) The NPS is continually reevaluating the pet policy. Be sure to follow the rules so that you don't ruin the visit for other hikers and pet owners or cause harm to your pet and wildlife.

Parking, camping, and fires are allowed only in designated spots. No camping is allowed in the backcountry, only in Seawall and Blackwoods Campgrounds. Blackwoods and Seawall are closed in winter. Firearms are prohibited in the park unless they are packed away or unless other exceptions under federal and Maine law apply, such as permitted concealed carry.

Safety and Preparation

Use caution near cliffs and water's edge, especially during stormy weather. People have been swept to sea by storm driven waves. Don't turn your back on the ocean.

Wear proper footwear, ideally hiking boots, especially for the more challenging hikes; sneakers or some other sturdy closed-toe, rubber-soled shoe may be suitable for the easiest hikes. Trails and rocks can be slippery, especially when wet. Loose gravel on rocks can also be dangerous. Most injuries come from falls while hiking or biking.

Carry at least 1 quart of water per person. Do not count on finding water on any hike, but if you must use natural water sources, treat with water purifiers or iodine tablets before consumption.

Wear sunscreen and protective clothing, especially a hat to protect against the potentially harmful effects of overexposure to the sun.

Dress in layers and pack rain gear so that you are prepared for changes in weather. Bring extra socks and clothing.

If you hike alone, tell a reliable person your hiking plan, especially if you will be hiking in the more remote areas. Stick to your plan when you are on the hike, and be sure to check in upon your return.

Do not leave valuables in your car.

Day Hiker Checklist

- Day pack
- Food
- First-aid kit
- Insect repellent

- Headlamp or flashlight
- Camera
- Binoculars
- Trail guide
- Detailed trail map
- Compass or GPS unit
- Signal mirror
- Toilet paper and zippered plastic bags
- Sun hat
- Cell phone for emergencies

Leave No Trace

Many of the trails in Acadia National Park are heavily used, particularly in the peak summer months and into September. We, as trail users and advocates, must be especially vigilant to make sure our passage leaves no lasting mark.

Follow these Leave No Trace principles:

Leave with everything you brought.
Leave no sign of your visit.
Leave the landscape as you found it.

And here are some additional guidelines for preserving trails in the park:

Pack out all your own trash, including biodegradable items like orange peels. You might also pack out garbage left by less considerate hikers.

Don't approach or feed any wild creatures—the ground squirrel eyeing your snack food is best able to survive if it remains self-reliant. Plus it's prohibited in the park.

- Don't pick wildflowers or gather rocks, shells, and other natural or historic features along the trail. Removing these items will only take away from the next hiker's experience. Plus it's prohibited in the park.
- Don't alter the cairns—piles of rocks that serve as trail markers—or create new ones.
- Avoid damaging trailside soils and plants by remaining on the established route.
- Walk single file in the center of the trail.
- Don't cut switchbacks, which can promote erosion.
- Be courteous by not making loud noises or casual cell phone calls while hiking.
- Many of these trails are shared with trail runners and dog walkers, and some are accessible to visitors with wheelchairs or baby strollers. Familiarize yourself with the proper trail etiquette, yielding the trail when appropriate.
- Use facilities at trailheads where available. Bury human waste in areas without toilets, and pack out toilet paper.
- Pick up after pets.

Visitor Information

Information about the park may be obtained by contacting Acadia National Park, PO Box 177, Bar Harbor 04609-0177. The telephone number is (207) 288-3338; the website is nps.gov/acad.

The Hulls Cove Visitor Center, which received an interior renovation in 2019, is located on ME 3, northwest Bar Harbor. Generally, it is open from 8:30 a.m. to 4:30 p.m. daily from early May through the end of October. Please check operating hours and seasons at nps.gov/acad.

planyourvisit/hours.htm. There is also a well-stocked book and gift store here run by the nonprofit Eastern National with its own entrance, created in the 2019 renovation.

A second welcome center for the park, the Acadia Gateway Center, is scheduled to open in 2025 on the west side of ME 3 in Trenton, with a goal of persuading more visitors to stop and get aboard the Island Explorer to the park. The Gateway Center is planned as a statewide information center and a regional transit hub with plenty of parking and expanded bus service to the park on the fare-free shuttle.

Winter visitor services for Acadia are shared with the Bar Harbor Chamber of Commerce at 2 Cottage Street, at the corner of Main Street, Bar Harbor. Hours are 8 a.m. to 4 p.m. daily from November through early May. Some hiking trails and parts of the 27-mile Park Loop Road are seasonally closed or may be closed for safety reasons or to protect nesting peregrine falcons. Check for trail and road closures with NPS officials or at nps.gov/acad.

Park entrance fees apply year-round, with a seven-day pass available for one vehicle; a seven-day pass for one individual on foot, motorcycle, or bicycle; and an annual pass for one vehicle. Passes may be purchased at recreation.gov, the visitor center, and other local sites.

From June 23 to Indigenous Peoples' Day (as the federal Columbus Day holiday is called in Maine), the fare-free Island Explorer bus operates between points on Mount Desert Island and the park. For schedules, routes, stops, and other information, go to exploreacadia.com.

Hikers also might find the National Geographic Acadia National Park Trails Illustrated Topographic Map helpful. You can go to natgeomaps.com/ti-212-acadia-national-park to get your Trails Illustrated map. Other maps and literature are available at the park's visitor center.

How to Use This Guide

This guide is designed to be simple and easy to use.

Each hike is described with a map and summary information that delivers the trail's vital statistics, including length, difficulty, and canine compatibility.

Directions to the trailhead are also provided, along with a general description of what you'll see along the way. A detailed route finder ("Miles and Directions") sets forth mileage between significant landmarks along the trail.

Trailhead GPS coordinates listed in the "Finding the trailhead" section of each hike description are based on data collected by us, provided by Acadia National Park, or gathered from other reliable sources, such as the website of the US Board on Geographic Names (usgs.gov/us-board-on -geographic-names). If your GPS uses a different notation than the one used here, you can convert data here: fcc.gov media/radio/dms-decimal.

But, as with any GPS data provided for recreational use, there are no warranties, expressed or implied, about data accuracy, completeness, reliability, or suitability. The data should *not* be used for primary navigation. Readers of this guide assume the entire risk as to the quality and use of the data.

Acadia National Park officials advise that visitors obey posted signs and park regulations, use common sense, and avoid accidentally traveling on private lands while using a GPS unit.

Difficulty Ratings

These are all easy hikes, but "easy" is a relative term. To aid in the selection of a hike that suits particular needs and abilities, each is rated easy, moderate, or more challenging. Bear in mind that even the most challenging routes can be made easy by hiking within your limits and taking rests when you need them.

- **Easy** hikes are generally short and flat, taking no longer than 1 to 2 hours to complete.

  Moderate hikes involve relatively mild changes in elevation and will take 1 to 2.5 hours to complete.

  More challenging hikes feature some steep stretches, greater distances, and generally take longer than 2.5 hours to complete.

These are completely subjective ratings—consider that what you think is easy is entirely dependent on your level of fitness and the adequacy of your gear (primarily shoes). If you are hiking with a group, you should select a hike with a rating that's appropriate for the least fit and prepared in your party.

Approximate hiking times are based on the assumption that on flat ground, most walkers average 2 miles per hour. Adjust that rate by the steepness and difficulty of the terrain and your level of fitness. Be sure to add more time if you plan to picnic or take part in other activities like bird-watching or photography.

Trail Finder

Best Hikes for Great Views

4	Cadillac Summit Loop Trail
5	Beachcroft Path
6	Champlain North Ridge Trail
8	Sand Beach and Great Head Trail
9	Ocean Path
11	Gorham Mountain Trail
16	Acadia Mountain Trail
17	Flying Mountain Trail
18	Beech Cliff Loop Trail

Best Hikes for Children

1	Bar Island Trail
2	Jesup Path and Hemlock Path Loop
4	Cadillac Summit Loop Trail
8	Sand Beach and Great Head Trail
9	Ocean Path
13	Jordan Stream Path
20	Wonderland
21	Ship Harbor Trail
22	Bass Harbor Head Light Trail

Best Hikes for Dogs

1	Bar Island Trail
3	Compass Harbor Trail
4	Cadillac Summit Loop Trail
7	Schooner Head Overlook and Path
13	Jordan Stream Path
18	Beech Cliff Loop Trail

Map Legend

——③——	State Highway
═══════	Local Road
= = = = = = =	Unpaved Road
▬▬▬▬▬▬	Featured Trail
- - - - - - - -	Trail
～～～	River/Creek
—·—·—·—	Intermittent Stream
⚶ ⚶	Marsh
▭	National Park
⛵	Boat Ramp
⏝	Bridge
Ⓐ	Campground
ⵑ	Lighthouse
▲	Mountain/Peak
🅿	Parking
🛆	Picnic Area
■	Point of Interest/Structure
⑪	Restaurant
🚻	Restroom
⚲	Spring
○	Town
⓫	Trailhead
▯	Tower
☎	Telephone
◖	Viewpoint
❓	Visitor/Information Center
≋	Waterfall

Mount Desert Island East of Somes Sound

Most of Acadia National Park's trails, the main Park Loop Road, and many of the best views are here on the eastern half of Mount Desert Island. Most f the "best easy" hikes are also located here.

The various hikes in this section are grouped into three eographic divisions: the Bar Harbor/Cadillac and Cham-lain Mountains area, the Gorham Mountain area, and the rdan Pond and Bubbles area.

From trails in the Bar Harbor/Cadillac and Champlain Mountains area, you can get some of Acadia's best-known ews of Bar Harbor, Frenchman Bay, and the Porcupine lands. The park's Sieur de Monts entrance is also here, lowing access to the Wild Gardens of Acadia, the Nature enter, and the Abbe Museum.

The Gorham Mountain area features such seashore hikes Sand Beach and Great Head Trail and the very easy Ocean th, as well as such moderate hikes as the Gorham Moun-n Trail.

A new trail for this fifth edition, Seaside Path, was ived by an extensive rehabilitation led by the Acadia trails w and reopened in 2020. Seaside Path links a public sand ch at Seal Harbor with Jordan Pond.

At the heart of the Jordan Pond and Bubbles area is Jordan Pond House, famous for its afternoon tea and popovers and its view of the twin peaks known as the Bubbles. The Jordan Pond House serves as a jumping-off point for an easy trail around the pond. Other dominant features accessible by trails in this area include a precariously perched rock known as Bubble Rock and one of Acadia's famed carriage road bridges, Cobblestone Bridge.

1 Bar Island Trail

A low-tide walk leads to a rocky island off Bar Harbor, providing a unique perspective back toward town and its mountain backdrop. The trail can also offer a close-up view of gulls feeding or starfish exposed by the tide.

Distance: 2.0 miles out and back
Hiking time: 1 to 1.5 hours
Difficulty: Easy
Trail surface: Low-tide gravel bar, gravel road, forest floor, rock ledges
Best season: Spring through fall, particularly early morning or late afternoon in summer to avoid the crowds
Other trail users: Trail runners, motorists on gravel bar

Canine compatibility: Leashed dogs permitted
Nat Geo Trails Illustrated Topographic Map: Acadia National Park
Special considerations: Accessible only 1.5 hours on either side of low tide. Check tide chart on Bar Island, in local newspapers, or at usharbors.com /harbor/maine/bar-harbor-me/ tides/. There is a public restroom at the intersection of West and Main Streets.

Finding the trailhead: From the park's visitor center, head south on ME 3 for about 2.5 miles, toward downtown Bar Harbor. Turn left (east) onto West Street at the first intersection after the College of the Atlantic. The trail, visible only at low tide, leaves from Bridge Street, the first left (north) off West Street on the edge of downtown. There is limited on-street paid parking with meters or kiosks on West Street. The closest Island Explorer stop is Bar Harbor Village Green. GPS: N44 23.30' / W68 12.35'

The Hike

The Bar Island Trail is a short, easy jaunt within shouting distance of Bar Harbor, but you feel transported to another world. That is the beauty of being on an island, even a small one like Bar Island, so close to a busy summer resort town itself located on an island.

It's easy enough for the least-seasoned hiker, with Dolores's mother, April, a first-time visitor to Acadia at 71 effortlessly strolling across. But the Bar Island Trail also provides a bit of risk to satisfy the thrill-seeking adventurer—it can be traveled only at low tide, when a gravel bar connecting Bar Harbor and the island is exposed. The incoming tide can quickly cover the bar and prevent people from hiking off the island.

"Time your hike carefully," a sign warns hikers once they reach the island's rocky shores. "The tide changes quickly. Plan to be off the bar no later than 1.5 hours after low tide lest you become stuck. For your convenience, a tide chart posted, as well as phone numbers for a water taxi and Acadia dispatch if a water taxi is unavailable. Don't become one of the visitors who periodically get stranded on the island or whose car get swamped while parked on the gravel bar.

First described in 1867, the trail was used by the rusticators, the popular name for visitors who came to Maine for extended summer vacations during the mid- to late nineteenth century.

It was closed for a certain period and then reopened the National Park Service in 1990, when the island was still partly privately owned. The NPS completed ownership of the island in 2003 when it purchased 12 acres from former *NBC News* correspondent Jack Perkins and his wife

Mary Jo, who lived for thirteen years in a small home they built there. Perkins, who died in 2019, called the island his "garden of Eden" and detailed his time there in his 2013 book, *Finding Moosewood, Finding God*. Maybe you can also discover God, or at least a sign of God, during a hike to the 0.5-mile-long island, as we perhaps did on a cloudless early evening in September 2017, when a bald eagle hovered for a while just above our heads near the start of the wooded island.

The hike begins at the foot of Bridge Street in Bar Harbor. Be forewarned: On a sunny summer weekend day or holiday, the walk can almost become circus-like, with big crowds and passing vehicles—and maybe one or two becoming stuck in the sand. For a more tranquil coastal trek, try early morning or late afternoon on a weekday for the low-tide hike.

Walk northwest across the gravel bar, catch a view of nearby Sheep Porcupine Island, and reach Bar Island at about 0.4 mile. Some of the resort town's historic summer "cottages"—really mansions—are visible along Bar Harbor's shoreline to the left (southwest) as you cross the gravel bar.

Please do not remove or stack cobbles at the base of the island at the end of the bar. A violation of Leave No Trace principles, rock stacking is an annoying form of vandalism that is increasingly marring open spaces across the country, and the NPS and Friends of Acadia are attempting to prevent it (or at least limit the stacking to inside the tide line so it can be washed away with the high tide).

Once you reach Bar Island, head northeast up the gravel road behind the gate. The trail soon levels off at a grassy field. At about 0.6 mile, bear left (northeast) at a trail sign pointing into the woods toward Bar Island summit. At a

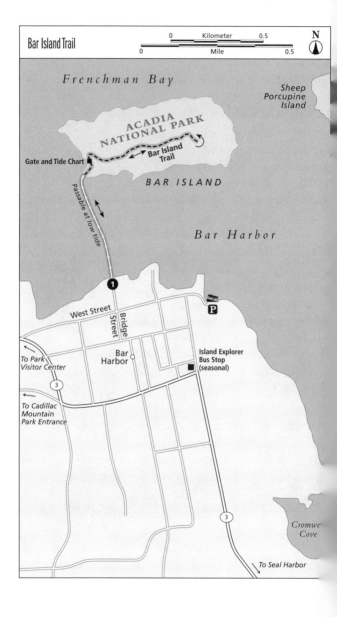

ork at about 0.8 mile, marked by a cairn (a pile of rocks to mark a change in trail direction), bear right (southeast) up a rocky knob.

At about 1.0 mile you reach the rocky summit, with its views toward Bar Harbor, as well as several Acadia peaks: from left to right, Champlain Mountain, Huguenot Head, and Dorr and Cadillac Mountains. From here you can hear the town's church bells, see the fishing and recreational boats along the harbor, and take in the smells of the sea and the views of the mountains.

Return the way you came.

Miles and Directions

0.0   Start at the Bar Island trailhead, at the foot of Bridge Street.

0.4   Reach the shore of Bar Island. Check the posted tide chart to time your return; otherwise you'll have to wait more than 12 hours for the next low tide. Head northeast up the gravel road behind the gate.

0.6   Cross a grassy field and come to a junction; bear left (northeast) into the woods at the trail sign.

0.8   Reach another junction marked by a cairn; bear right (southeast) up to the island's summit.

1.0   Reach the island's summit, with views back toward Bar Harbor and the mountains.

2.0   Arrive back at the trailhead.

2 Jesup Path and Hemlock Path Loop

This woods and wetlands walk takes you by Sieur de Monts Spring and the rehabilitated Spring Pool, the Wild Gardens of Acadia, the Nature Center, and the Abbe Museum. You'll hear birdsong and get open views of Huguenot Head and the Champlain and Dorr Mountains along Great Meadow. You may even catch sight of deer, a pileated woodpecker, or baby barred owls.

Distance: 1.6-mile figure-eight loop

Hiking time: About 1 hour

Difficulty: Easy

Trail surface: Forest floor, graded gravel path, wooden boardwalk and bridges

Best season: Spring through fall, particularly early morning or late afternoon in summer to avoid the crowds

Other trail users: Dog walkers, trail runners, area residents

Canine compatibility: Leashed dogs permitted (but not in the Wild Gardens of Acadia, Nature Center, or Abbe Museum)

Nat Geo Trails Illustrated Topographic Map: Acadia National Park

Special considerations: Graded gravel and wooden boardwalk surfaces make part of the walk wheelchair and baby-stroller accessible. Seasonal restrooms are available at the Sieur de Monts parking area.

Finding the trailhead: From downtown Bar Harbor, head south on ME 3 for about 2 miles, turn right (northwest) into the park's Sieur de Monts entrance, and then make a quick left (west) into the Sieur de Monts parking area. From the parking area, cross the wooden bridge between the Nature Center and Wild Gardens of Acadia to find the trailhead, marked by a sign that says "To Jesup Path," and head right (northwest) to start the loop. The Island Explorer stops at Sieur de Monts. GPS for parking area: N44 21.47' / W68 12.33'

icked out by our niece Michelle as her birthday hike one
ear, this was a perfect walk for three generations of the
mily, ranging from 82-year-old April to 13-year-old Jenna.
Ve toured the Wild Gardens of Acadia at the start and, to
p it off, caught sight of deer and a pileated woodpecker
ong the loop, as the possibility of spotting wildlife was why
lichelle chose this to celebrate her 26th birthday.

Aside from the family memories, other reasons this is a
vorite hike of ours: the chance to see baby barred owls in
ringtime, walk through what must be Acadia's most-pho-
graphed birch grove, and take in the history and exhibits
the Sieur de Monts area.

Jesup Path was first created more than one hundred years
o by George B. Dorr and others as part of a garden path
t connected downtown Bar Harbor to Sieur de Monts
d its network of trails, as early twentieth-century rustica-
s—artists, tourists, and summer residents—would think
thing of walking 5, 10, or 15 miles a day from town to
untains, ponds, or sea.

Sieur de Monts is where Acadia all began in 1916 as a
ional monument, with Dorr as its first superintendent.

Another reason for the area's significance: It borders the
-acre Great Meadow Wetland, which, ironically, was
impacted by the early path- and road-building by Dorr
others that it is now the focus of a major restoration to
viate flooding and improve the health of the ecosystem.

Backed by $500,000 from the 2021 Bipartisan Infra-
cture Law, support from the Friends of Acadia and other
ips, and wetland restoration efforts by members of the
obscot, Passamaquoddy, Micmac, and Maliseet Tribes,

the multiyear project calls for removal of invasive plant
planting of native species likely to thrive in a changing cli
mate; improvement of water flow; and upgrades to the Grea
Meadow Loop and parts of the Jesup Path and Hemloc
Path Loop to create a more flood-resistant and accessible tra
system between Bar Harbor and Sieur de Monts.

To start the hike, cross the wooden bridge locate
between the Nature Center and Wild Gardens of Acadi
Follow the sign that points "To Jesup Path" and head rig
(northwest) to start the figure-eight loop hike along t
well-graded path.

At 0.1 mile reach the boardwalk portion of Jesup Pat
where you'll find wayside exhibits describing things
look for in the freshwater wetland you're traversing, su
as white paint lichen on rocks below and old man's bea
another type of lichen, hanging on branches above. The
are convenient benches to rest along the boardwalk.

At 0.4 mile, reach the northern end of the boardwa
Bear right (northeast) and then a quick left (northwest)
continue on a well-graded gravel portion of Jesup Pa
which takes you along Great Meadow to the Park Lo
Road. During severe flooding in the spring of 2023, so
of the wooden footbridges you see along this stretch of
path floated away and had to be retrieved and resecured
the trails crew.

As you head into the wide-open portion of the G
Meadow, turn around and look back to take in the v
of Champlain to the left (east) and Dorr to the right (we

Continue northwest and reach the Park Loop Roa
0.7 mile. Turn right (east) onto a rerouted section of
Great Meadow Loop to connect with Hemlock Path in
mile, thus forming the top of the figure-eight loop of

ike. This reroute is part of the Great Meadow Wetland estoration and means hikers no longer need to cross the ine-way Park Loop Road to walk a short spell along the old oute of the Great Meadow Loop before recrossing the road o pick up Hemlock Path.

At 0.8 mile, turn right (southwest) onto Hemlock Path nd reach the much-photographed birch grove at 0.9 mile, ith views of Champlain Mountain and Huguenot Head to ie left (east).

To improve water flow through the Great Meadow Jetland along this section of trail, and to make it more ccessible for visitors with wheelchairs or baby strollers, the irk plans to build 500 feet of boardwalk and make other ibgrades as part of the major Great Meadow restoration.

At 1.0 mile, circle back to the northern end of the Jesup ith boardwalk, which comes in on the left. Stay straight on emlock Path and at a three-way junction at 1.1 miles, with ratheden Path coming in on the right and the rougher emlock Trail ahead, turn left (southeast) to continue on e well-graded Hemlock Path.

What's notable about this section of the path that was ce a road, as we learned on a ranger-led nature walk here e year: During the great fire of 1947 that burned more in 10,000 acres in Acadia, the road served as a firebreak that the original evergreen trees to the right (west) sur- ed, while those on the left (east) burned and have been ceeded by the deciduous trees that now make Acadia's foliage so brilliant.

At 1.5 miles, reach the junction with the southern end the Jesup Path boardwalk, closing the figure-eight loop. rn right (southeast) and return to the start at 1.6 miles.

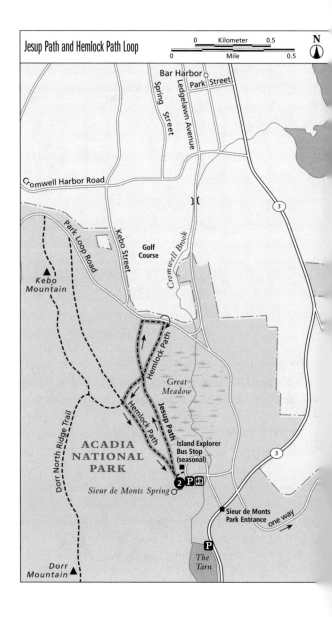

Jesup Path and Hemlock Path Loop

N

Kilometer 0.5

Mile 0.5

Bar Harbor

Park Street

Spring Street

Ledgelawn Avenue

Cromwell Harbor Road

3

Park Loop Road

Kebo Street

Golf Course

Cromwell Brook

Kebo Mountain

Hemlock Path

Great Meadow

Dorr North Ridge Trail

Hemlock Path

Jesup Path

ACADIA NATIONAL PARK

Island Explorer Bus Stop (seasonal)

2

Sieur de Monts Spring

3

Sieur de Monts Park Entrance

one way

Dorr Mountain

P

The Tarn

From here, if you choose, you can stop in at the Nature Center or gardens; visit the Sieur de Monts Spring Canopy and Spring Pool; or, if open for the season, see the original site of the Abbe Museum (a Smithsonian–affiliated institution focusing on the Wabanaki Nations' heritage, culture, and homelands) and a wigwam where Native American cultural demonstrations may be held.

Miles and Directions

0.0 Start at the Jesup Path trailhead on the other side of a wooden bridge, located between the Nature Center and Wild Gardens of Acadia, and head right (northwest).

0.1 Continue on the boardwalk section of Jesup Path.

0.4 At the end of the boardwalk, bear right (northeast), and then take a quick left (northwest) to continue on a well-graded gravel portion of Jesup Path.

0.7 Reach the northern end of Jesup Path at the Park Loop Road and turn right (east) onto a rerouted section of the Great Meadow Loop.

0.8 Complete the top of the figure-eight loop; turn right (southwest) onto Hemlock Path.

0.9 Walk through the birch grove.

1.0 Circle back to the northern end of the Jesup Path boardwalk that comes in on the left; stay straight on Hemlock Path.

1.1 At a three-way junction, with Stratheden Path coming in on the right and the rougher Hemlock Trail ahead, turn left (southeast) to stay on the well-graded Hemlock Path.

1.5 Reach the southern end of the Jesup Path boardwalk, closing the figure-eight loop, and turn right (southeast).

1.6 Arrive back at the trailhead.

3 Compass Harbor Trail

Situated just outside Bar Harbor, this easy trail offers both important history—it's the former site of park pioneer George B. Dorr's Oldfarm estate—and sweeping ocean and island views, with its point right on Frenchman Bay. The trail features some remnants of Dorr's family home, older growth trees, Dorr Point, and sights along the bay.

Distance: 0.8 mile out and back
Hiking time: About 30 minutes
Difficulty: Easy
Trail surface: Gravel road, forest floor, sandy trail at end
Best season: Spring through fall, particularly off-peak times
Other trail users: Dog walkers, trail runners, area residents
Canine compatibility: Leashed dogs permitted

Nat Geo Trails Illustrated Topographic Map: Acadia National Park
Special considerations: No facilities. An Oldfarm app, produced by the park and Northern Arizona University to educate visitors, is used with an Apple device in tandem with 11 numbered stations along the trail.

Finding the trailhead: From downtown Bar Harbor head south on ME 3 for 1 mile. A small parking lot is located on the left (east) just after Nannau Wood, a private road, and just before Old Farm Road, also private. The trail begins off the parking lot. If the parking lot is full (often the case during peak times), you can park at the town ball fields and walk south just over 0.5 mile along ME 3 to the trailhead. The closest Island Explorer bus stop is at Bar Harbor Village Green. GPS: N44 22.25' / W68 11.51'

At Compass Harbor you can see where the park's first super-intendent, George B. Dorr, took his daily swim in the cold waters of Frenchman Bay or tended to the wide-ranging gardens that once surrounded his sprawling estate here, called Oldfarm. The trail begins as a wide gravel road off the parking lot and soon comes to a sign pointing to Compass Harbor. The trail goes left and narrows as it approaches the ocean.

During a hike with now-retired ranger Maureen Fournier, an authority on Compass Harbor, she noted that the trail partly utilizes a roadbed from a formal driveway to the mansion, which was considered the first well-built estate in Bar Harbor.

"Imagine going back in time one hundred years to see what this was like," said Fournier, who once conducted the park's interpretive program at Compass Harbor.

Head out on a sandy trail on a peninsula toward Dorr Point, but stop before an eroded section of the trail that became even more eroded from a devastating rainstorm in early January 2024. Compass Harbor and Ogden Point are located to the left (north and northwest), and Sols Cliff is to the right (southeast). Frenchman Bay is straight ahead.

Near the point, look for some old granite blocks that were once part of Dorr's saltwater bathing pool that filled at high tide.

Just before reaching the point, an unofficial trail leads to the ruins of the Dorr manor house, which was built from 1880 to 1881 on land purchased by his father in 1868 and donated to the National Park Service by Dorr in 1942.

We counted forty-three granite steps and came upon a[n] aged foundation for the Oldfarm manor house and a bric[k] patio.

"It is widely believed this is granite from his ow[n] quarry," which was owned by the family and located at th[e] southern end of the estate, Fournier said. "The steps all com[e] from his quarry."

In 2016 the NPS completed a 145-page *Cultural Land[scape Inventory and Assessment for Oldfarm]*, which recommen[ds] management approaches for the 58 acres the park still ow[ns] from the original 100-acre estate at Compass Harbor an[d] analyzes the historical significance of the property.

None of Dorr's formal gardens remain, but several plan[ts] and shrubs from the historic period can still be found [at] the manor site, Fournier said, including a large lilac and [a] prominent vine.

An arborvitae hedge, which likely separated a ten[nis] court from the cutting garden, has deteriorated, but abo[ut] ten to twelve trees still exist, per the NPS assessment.

Dorr was adamant that his cherished Oldfarm beco[me] part of the park and even offered the property as a su[m]mer White House to President Calvin Coolidge in 19[__] and then to the executive branch under President Frank[lin] D. Roosevelt in 1940 to garner support, according to [the] assessment.

Roosevelt suggested that it be donated to the N[PS] and the property finally became part of the park two ye[ars] before Dorr died at Oldfarm. But in 1951, finding the est[ate] too expensive to preserve and maintain, the NPS razed [it,] Fournier said.

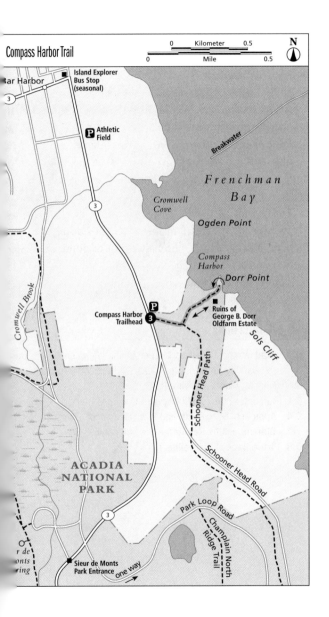

Compass Harbor Trail

0   Kilometer   0.5
0   Mile   0.5

N

Island Explorer
Bus Stop
(seasonal)

Bar Harbor

3

Athletic
Field

Breakwater

*Frenchman
Bay*

Cromwell
Cove

Ogden Point

*Compass
Harbor*

Dorr Point

Cromwell Brook

Compass Harbor
Trailhead

3

Ruins of
George B. Dorr
Oldfarm Estate

Sols Cliff

Schooner Head Path

ACADIA
NATIONAL
PARK

Schooner Head Road

3

Park Loop Road

Champlain North
Ridge Trail

Sieur de Monts
Park Entrance

one way

r de
onts
ring

"People are aghast when you tell them what happened with the house, but it was 1951, and the NPS had no money," she explained.

At that time in the nation's history, in the wake of the Great Depression and World War II, one can imagine that the federal government didn't have the funds to keep up Oldfarm or many other facilities or programs.

The estate's 1879 Storm Beach Cottage, where Dorr often stayed, is still in good condition and is used as part staff housing.

Today the NPS calls Dorr the father of the park and credits him for his indefatigable work in leading the effort to create Acadia. There's no better spot to ponder that topic than Compass Harbor.

Return the way you came.

Miles and Directions

0.0 Start at the Compass Harbor trailhead, which leaves from the parking lot on the left (east) side of ME 3, just south of Nannau Wood, a private road.

0.1 Turn left at the junction toward Compass Harbor.

0.4 Approach Dorr Point and the remains of George B. Dorr Oldfarm estate. Return the way you came.

0.8 Arrive back at the trailhead.

Cadillac Summit Loop Trail

ated at the top of Acadia's highest mountain, this short easy trail offers maybe the best views in the park and yside exhibits that identify more than forty islands, peaks, other key points that lie off its slopes. On a sunny day loop is the best place for any hiker to get some bearings ore exploring the rest of Acadia. The trail is often busy ing peak summer months, since cars and buses can drive the mountain's access road. In order to eliminate traffic gestion, a paid vehicle reservation system for the summit d took effect during the 2021 season.

ance: 0.3-mile loop

ng time: About 30 minutes

iculty: Easy

surface: Paved walkway

t season: Spring through fall, icularly early morning or late rnoon in summer to avoid the ds

er trail users: Hikers coming Gorge Path or Cadillac North e or Cadillac South Ridge s, visitors with wheelchairs or y strollers, birders

ine compatibility: Leashed s permitted

Geo Trails Illustrated graphic Map: Acadia onal Park

Special considerations: The walkway is partially accessible for visitors with wheelchairs or baby strollers, just the short distance from the parking lot to a viewing platform. The 3.5-mile paved auto road to the summit is a winding and narrow route. There is a seasonal summit gift shop and restrooms. In addition to the park's entrance pass, a vehicle reservation (minimal fee) is required from about the end of May to late October, available at recreation.gov.

Finding the trailhead: From the park's visitor center, drive south on the Park Loop Road for about 3.5 miles and turn left (east) at the sign for Cadillac Mountain. Ascend the winding summit road to the top. The paved walkway begins off the eastern side of the parking lot, across from the summit gift shop. The Island Explorer bus does not go up Cadillac, but there is a Cadillac North Ridge stop, where the 2.2-mile moderately difficult Cadillac North Ridge Trail takes you to the top and a connection with the Cadillac Summit Loop Trail. GPS: N44 21.09' / W68 13.28'

The Hike

You gain a new appreciation for 1,530-foot-high Cadillac Mountain on this trail, with wayside exhibits describing the history and features of Mount Desert Island and the panoramic views from the highest point on the East Coast of the United States.

The 0.3-mile summit loop trail on the peak includes two viewing platforms and excellent vistas of the Porcupine and Cranberry Islands, Frenchman Bay, Great Head, the Beehive, Otter Point, and Dorr and other mountains. It's the quintessential family hike, simple and inspiring for visitors of any age.

Our cousins, Melissa Kong-Buzzell and John Buzzell of Staten Island, New York, and their children, Tyler, then 10, and Amelia, 8, met us on the Cadillac summit for a hike in early August and found it an ideal way to start an Acadia vacation.

It was their first time on the peak, and Amelia summed it up best for the family. "My favorite part is the view," she said. "I rate it a ten out of ten."

"This is the gift of Mother Nature," Tyler added. "We get to spend time together and we also get to experience that nature offers."

Near the start of the trail off the parking lot, a bronze memorial plaque, installed in 1932, commemorates Stephen Tyng Mather, a wealthy entrepreneur, leading advocate for the creation of the National Park Service in 1916, and its first director.

Newly designed wayside exhibits, erected in 2015 along the trail and the edge of the parking lot, describe significant aspects of the area, including the geological essence of Acadia—the pink granite with its three main minerals; the night sky over Acadia; and the visionaries who helped found the park a century ago, from George B. Dorr to Charles Eliot and John D. Rockefeller Jr.

A top feature of this hike is a circular platform with two exhibits that pinpoint about forty highlights of the sweeping views, allowing anyone to find spots such as Turtle Island, Egg Rock, Schoodic Point, Porcupine Islands, Seawall Campground, Baker Island, Little Cranberry Island, and the Gulf of Maine.

Aside from the islands and other sites, you may also hear song sparrows during the spring or see bald eagles and turkey vultures soaring above Cadillac, especially during the annual HawkWatch from late August through mid-October, when migrating raptors such as kestrels, peregrine falcons, and sharp-shinned hawks can be spotted.

You may also see three-toothed cinquefoil, lowbush blueberries, a tiny white flower known as mountain sandwort, and the pink blooms of rhodora. Even a couple of small birch trees can be found along the walkway, proof of the success of restoration efforts over the past decade or so. Wooden barricades and signs reminding hikers to stay on the trail and solid rock are part of the continued revegetation program in the wake of uncontrolled trampling in the past that caused erosion and changed the appearance of the area.

Don't look for a peak sign off the trail. The peak of Cadillac, as marked by the US Geological Survey, is actually off the Cadillac South Ridge Trail, near an antenna behind the gift shop, but the best views are from the loop trail.

There are two access points to the paved summit loop trail off the eastern edge of the parking area. The access point on the left (northeast), near the accessible parking spots, is also the start of a paved path that can be used by those with physical disabilities and people with baby strollers to reach the main viewing platform without climbing stairs.

The trail, started by the NPS in 1932 and completed the following year by the Civilian Conservation Corps—the Depression-era public work relief program—is a blend of concrete and crushed native pink Cadillac Mountain granite. It features several sets of granite boulders for steps, and even though the trail is easy, watch your footing; people have been injured along the walkway, which can be uneven in spots.

The road to the summit, finished in 1932 by the NPS, was among the first motor roads built in the park. Before the road was built, an entrepreneur constructed a cog railway in 1883 to the peak from Eagle Lake, but it was dismantled to years later because people generally preferred to escape the industrial age by hiking or taking a horse-drawn buckboard to the peak.

Because of its grand vistas and easy access, the trail can get very crowded in summer. Sunrise is a huge draw, part because Cadillac Mountain is the first place in the United States where the sun's rays hit between October 7 and March 6, generally, and nearly first the rest of the year. Sunsets can also be spectacular, best watched from a west-facing rock face overlooking Eagle Lake, off the secondary parking lot below the summit.

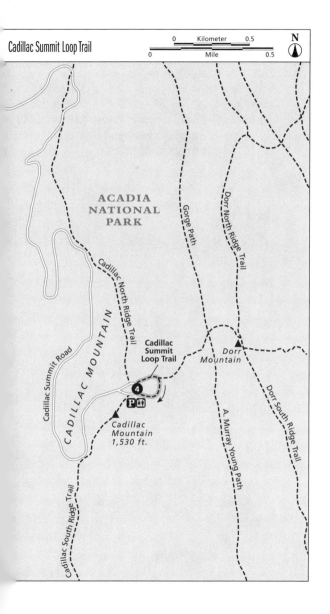

Kilometer

0   0.5

Mile

0   0.5

N

ACADIA
NATIONAL
PARK

Gorge Path

Dorr North Ridge Trail

Cadillac North Ridge Trail

Cadillac Summit Road

CADILLAC MOUNTAIN

Cadillac
Summit
Loop Trail

4

P

Cadillac
Mountain
1,530 ft.

Dorr
Mountain

A Murray Young Path

Dorr South Ridge Trail

Cadillac South Ridge Trail

Miles and Directions

0.0 Start at the Cadillac Summit Loop trailhead, with two access points located at the eastern edge of the parking area, across from the summit gift shop. The left (northeastern) trail entrance connects to a ramp that allows wheelchair and baby stroller access to a circular viewing area.

0.3 Complete the loop back at the trailhead.

5 Beachcroft Path

ntricately laid stone steps lead much of the way to open
iews along Huguenot Head, on the shoulder of Champlain
Mountain. In line with its more-than-a-century-old history,
nis route's name is reverting to the original description as
 path, rather than a trail, to better characterize its highly
onstructed nature. It's a mostly moderate ascent to this
ike's goal, but there's an option to climb more strenuously
r another 0.5 mile to reach the summit of Champlain and
s ocean views.

stance: 1.4 miles out and back
king time: 1 to 1.5 hours
fficulty: Moderate to more
allenging
il surface: Granite steps, rock
dges, forest floor
st season: Spring through fall
her trail users: None
nine compatibility: Leashed
s permitted

**Nat Geo Trails Illustrated
Topographic Map:** Acadia
National Park
Special considerations: If you
tack on the stretch to the top
of Champlain, be aware that
the steep section is not recommended for dogs. There are
no facilities at the trailhead.
Seasonal restrooms are at the
nearby Sieur de Monts park
entrance.

ding the trailhead: From downtown Bar Harbor head south on ME
r about 2.2 miles, just past the park's Sieur de Monts entrance,
ne parking lot on the right (west) just before the glacially carved
 known as the Tarn. The trailhead is on the left (east) side of ME 3,
ss the road diagonally (southeast) from the parking lot. Be careful
sing ME 3. The closest Island Explorer stop is Sieur de Monts.
: N44 21.30' / W68 12.19'

The Hike

The Beachcroft Path climbs to the shoulder of Huguenot Head, with an average elevation gain of 100 feet each 0. mile, but at times it feels remarkably like a walk along a garden path. The gradual switchbacks and neatly laid stepping stones turn what would otherwise be a vertical scramble int a gentler ascent.

Adding to the wonder are the constant open view toward Frenchman Bay, Dorr Mountain, the Cranber Isles, Champlain Mountain, and the Tarn.

Dome-shaped Huguenot Head, visible from Bar Harbc has been a popular destination for more than a centur The Beachcroft Path, built and rebuilt in the late 1800s ar early 1900s, was named for the estate of Bar Harbor sun mer resident Anna Smith, who financed its construction ar endowed the trail in 1926. It consists of hundreds of han hewn stepping stones and countless switchbacks. When was originally constructed by George B. Dorr and the E Harbor Village Improvement Association, the path began Sieur de Monts Spring, but the path's start had to be mov because of road construction.

From the trailhead across from the Tarn parking an ascend via the switchbacks and stone steps, catching yc breath on the plentiful level sections along the way. But careful—even the flattest-looking rock along the path be loose—and watch your step as you travel on open ro ledges.

With its crafted stonework and magnificent views, path might very well have been among Dorr's favori There is an iconic photo of him in front of a distinc large granite boulder, left foot forward, with stepping stc

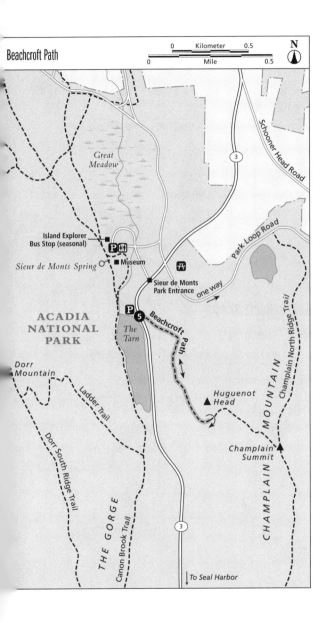

0   Kilometer   0.5

0   Mile   0.5

N

Great Meadow

3

Schooner Head Road

Park Loop Road

Island Explorer
Bus Stop (seasonal)

P

Sieur de Monts Spring

Museum

Sieur de Monts
Park Entrance

one way

P 5 Beachcroft Path

ACADIA
NATIONAL
PARK

The Tarn

Dorr Mountain

Ladder Trail

Dorr South Ridge Trail

Beachcroft Path

Huguenot Head

CHAMPLAIN MOUNTAIN

Champlain North Ridge Trail

Champlain Summit

THE GORGE

Canon Brook Trail

3

To Seal Harbor

stretching behind him. The boulder is so large, it is visible from along the shoreline of the Tarn, and so recognizable it is easy to find about 0.3 mile up Beachcroft Path. You can strike the same pose as Dorr and channel "the father of Acadia."

Near the shoulder of Huguenot Head, the path widens and levels off. It circles to the northeast as you reach the open ledge just below the head's summit, ending at 0.7 mile with views south toward the Cranberry Isles. To the east (left) is Champlain Mountain; to the west (right) is Dorr Mountain. Down below are the Tarn and ME 3.

Return the way you came. Ambitious hikers can continue east toward the summit of Champlain Mountain, a more challenging additional 0.5-mile climb.

Miles and Directions

0.0 Start at the Beachcroft Path trailhead, diagonally (southeast) across ME 3 from the parking lot that's just south of the Sieur de Monts park entrance.

0.7 Reach the open ledge on the shoulder of Huguenot Head and enjoy the views. Return the way you came.

1.4 Arrive back at the trailhead.

6 Champlain North Ridge Trail

Enjoy expansive views from the summit of Champlain Mountain and all along the open ridge, the closest to the ocean of all of Acadia's ridges. At times you'll see the contrast of fog rolling in over Frenchman Bay below and sun shining overhead, or storm clouds streaming in from the west as clear skies still prevail to the east.

Distance: 2.0 miles out and back
Hiking time: 1.5 to 2 hours
Difficulty: Moderate to more challenging
Trail surface: Rock ledges, forest floor
Best season: Spring through fall
Other trail users: None

Canine compatibility: Leashed dogs permitted
Nat Geo Trails Illustrated Topographic Map: Acadia National Park
Special considerations: No facilities at trailhead; seasonal restrooms at nearby Bear Brook picnic area

Finding the trailhead: Enter the park at the Sieur de Monts entrance, which is about 2 miles south of downtown Bar Harbor on ME 3. Turn right (south) onto the one-way Park Loop Road. The trailhead is 0.8 mile from the entrance, on the right (south) after the Bear Brook picnic area. There is a small parking area on the left (north), across the road just beyond the trailhead. The closest Island Explorer stop is Sieur de Monts, but it's a bit of a walk, so you may want to ask whether the bus driver can let you off at the trailhead. GPS: N44 21.47' / W68 11.36'

The Hike

On the Champlain North Ridge Trail early one morning, a blanket of fog rolled in and enveloped the Porcupine Islands

in the space of a few minutes. Amazingly, the ridgetop tra
continued to be bathed in sunshine as the foghorns sounde
their warnings below.

Another time, we started a late afternoon walk und
sunny skies, but by the time we got to the summit a mi
away, strong rain forced us to put on full storm gear from hea
to toe. It was sunny once again as we returned to the trailhea

Contrasts like these are part of the very nature of Acadi
where the mountains meet the sea and the weather can va
from moment to moment.

The trail, formerly known as the Bear Brook Tra
until it was restored to its historic name by the park, offe
spectacular views from Frenchman Bay to Great Head as
climbs the northern ridge of 1,058-foot Champlain Mou
tain. This is one of the oldest marked trails on Mount Des
Island, showing up on 1890s maps, when Champlain us
to be known as Newport Mountain. The Civilian Conse
vation Corps rerouted the lower, northern end of the tr
in the 1930s during construction of a motor road for t
now-abandoned Bear Brook Campground, according to t
National Park Service report on the historic Mount Des
Island Trail System.

From the trailhead head south and start ascendi
through a birch grove. The trail levels off a bit at about (
mile and then ascends more steeply up some stone steps.

The junction with the Orange & Black Path (forme
known as the East Face Trail) is at 0.4 mile. Contin
straight (south) and climb a steep pink-granite face. Foll
blue blazes and Bates-style cairns (artfully placed groups
four to six rocks that point the way) as you near the summ

As part of staying true to the history of Acadia's tra
the Bates cairns, pioneered by Waldron Bates, chair of

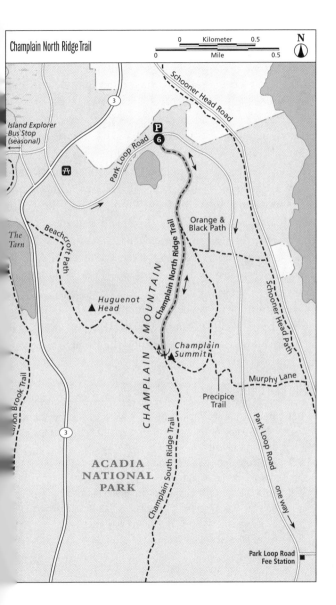

Champlain North Ridge Trail

Island Explorer
Bus Stop
(seasonal)

Park Loop Road

The
Tarn

Beachcroft Path

Huguenot
Head

Orange &
Black Path

Champlain North Ridge Trail

CHAMPLAIN MOUNTAIN

Champlain
Summit

Schooner Head Road

Schooner Head Path

Murphy Lane

Precipice
Trail

Park Loop Road

Champlain South Ridge Trail

ACADIA
NATIONAL
PARK

one way

Park Loop Road
Fee Station

Roads and Paths Committee of the Bar Harbor Village
Improvement Association from 1900 to 1909, have replaced
conical piles of rocks and supplement blue blazes as trail
markers, particularly on ridgelines on the east side of Mount
Desert Island. Don't move, add, or take away rocks from the
seemingly Zen-like Bates cairns. They are designed with a
purpose, with the gap in the base and the top stone pointing in the right direction. Any alteration can wreak havoc
for other hikers, never mind for those maintaining the trails.

At 1.0 mile reach the Champlain summit, with the closest mountaintop views of Frenchman Bay and the Porcupine Islands in all of Acadia. Boasting a sweeping outlook
to the east, the peak is an excellent alternative to Cadillac
for watching sunrise. You also reach the junction with the
Precipice and Champlain South Ridge Trails and the upper
Beachcroft Path at the summit.

Return the way you came. Intrepid hikers can continue
down the Champlain South Ridge Trail for another 1
miles to a mountain pond known as the Bowl.

Miles and Directions

0.0 Start at the Champlain North Ridge trailhead, on the right
(south) side of the one-way Park Loop Road, after the Bear
Brook picnic area.
0.4 Reach the junction with the Orange & Black Path. Continue
straight on the main trail.
1.0 Arrive at the Champlain Mountain summit and the junction
with the Precipice and Champlain South Ridge Trails and the
upper Beachcroft Path. Return the way you came.
2.0 Arrive back at the trailhead.

7 Schooner Head Overlook and Path

Sample a unique Acadia experience by walking along recently reopened historic trails from a spectacular shore overlook to the base of Champlain's cliffs, with options for longer treks. Along the way you'll pass through deciduous forest and by grand cliff views, and you can imagine what it was like when nineteenth-century rusticators traveled these same footpaths.

Distance: 2.0 miles out and back

Hiking time: 1 to 1.5 hours

Difficulty: Easy

Trail surface: Forest floor, graded gravel path, wooden bridge

Best season: Spring through fall

Other trail users: Trail runners, dog walkers, area residents

Canine compatibility: Leashed dogs permitted

Nat Geo Trails Illustrated Topographic Map: Acadia National Park

Special considerations: No facilities at trailhead

Finding the trailhead: From the park's visitor center, drive south on the Park Loop Road for about 3 miles; turn left (east) at the sign for Sand Beach. Follow the one-way Park Loop Road for about 5 miles. Turn left (east) just before the park entrance station and head straight for 0.2 mile, across Schooner Head Road, to the Schooner Head Overlook parking lot. The trailhead is just beyond the northwest corner of the parking lot, before the exit to Schooner Head Road. There is no nearby Island Explorer stop, but the bus passes through the nearby park entrance station, and you may ask the bus driver to let you off there if it is safe to do so. GPS: N44 20.22' / W68 10.44'

The Hike

Where else but in Acadia can you go from shore to cliff in just a mile? And also step through time?

Start off by taking in the oceanfront views at Schooner Head Overlook, at the easternmost end of the parking lot. To the north (left) is the rocky peninsula known as Schooner Head, and out in Frenchman Bay is Egg Rock, with its lighthouse. As of 2014, with the clearing of trees and restoration of historic vistas, the precipice of Champlain Mountain is once again visible to the northwest.

Head just beyond the northwest corner of the parking lot and pick up Schooner Head Path, a recently reopened historic route. While the hike described here is along only a portion of Schooner Head Path, you can still imagine yourself a modern-day rusticator, seeing some of the same views that Hudson River School artists like Thomas Cole and Frederic Church saw or that George B. Dorr, regarded as the father of Acadia, fought so hard to protect. The path, first built in 1901, reopened with funds from the Acadia Trails Forever initiative and the private Fore River Foundation. It is a cooperative effort of the National Park Service, Friends of Acadia, area residents, the town of Bar Harbor, and nearby Jackson Laboratory.

Follow the well-graded and slightly hilly path through the woods for 0.1 mile; then cross Schooner Head Road, watching out for traffic, and pick up the trail as it continues on the other side. The path eventually levels off and parallels Schooner Head Road, taking you over a wooden bridge built over the outlet of a pond at 0.2 mile. Take in the grand views of the Champlain cliffs, your destination on this hike.

At 0.7 mile turn left (west) onto Murphy Lane, another reopened historic trail that was once open to horses and known as the Blue Path, showing up on maps dating back to the 1890s and serving as the main entrance to the Precipice before the Park Loop Road was constructed, according to the NPS report on the historic Mount Desert Island Trail System. Follow Murphy Lane straight (west) through the woods, and don't be confused by old trails that may criss-cross in spots.

At 1.0 mile cross the one-way Park Loop Road (look right for traffic) and arrive at the base of Champlain's cliffs, at the Precipice parking area. The Precipice Trail begins here, but it is one of the most difficult cliff climbs in Acadia and not suitable for novices or people afraid of heights. If the trail and Precipice parking area are closed for peregrine falcon nesting season, you can participate in a peregrine watch with park rangers, interns, and volunteers who set up spotting scopes in the parking area.

When we hiked this trail with 7-year-old Henry Fournier and his grandmother, retired Acadia National Park Ranger Maureen Fournier, we were impressed by this budding young birder. Even without referring to the birding book he had in hand, or the bird ID app his grandmother was using, Henry was able to identify the song of the black-throated green warbler echoing through the woods of Murphy Lane.

And as we arrived at the peregrine watch at the Precipice parking area, Henry looked through the spotting scope at an adult peregrine falcon on the cliff above and noted, "It looks like it's brushing off its feathers or something." Sure enough, it was observing falcon preening behavior, explained the raptor intern on duty.

Return the way you came.

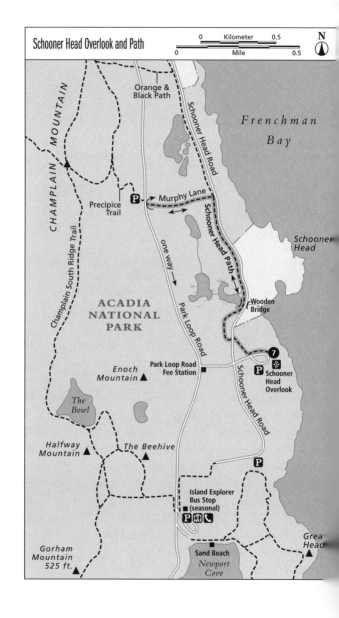

Schooner Head Overlook and Path

Kilometer 0 0.5
Mile 0 0.5

N

Frenchman Bay

Orange & Black Path

Schooner Head Road

CHAMPLAIN MOUNTAIN

Murphy Lane

Precipice Trail

Champlain South Ridge Trail

Schooner Head

one way

Schooner Head Path

ACADIA NATIONAL PARK

Wooden Bridge

Park Loop Road

Enoch Mountain ▲

Park Loop Road Fee Station ■

Schooner Head Road

7

Schooner Head Overlook

The Bowl

Halfway Mountain ▲

The Beehive ▲

Island Explorer Bus Stop ■ (seasonal)

Gorham Mountain 525 ft. ▲

Sand Beach ■
Newport Cove

*Grea
Head*

Miles and Directions

0.0 Start at the Schooner Head Path trailhead, just beyond the northwest corner of the Schooner Head Overlook parking lot, before the exit to Schooner Head Road.

0.1 Cross Schooner Head Road and continue on the path on the other (west) side of the road.

0.2 Cross a wooden bridge over the outlet of a pond, with views toward the Champlain cliffs.

0.7 Reach a junction with Murphy Lane. Turn left (west) and stay straight on the woods trail.

1.0 Cross the one-way Park Loop Road (look right for traffic) to reach the base of the Champlain cliffs at the Precipice parking area. Participate in a peregrine watch if it's peregrine falcon nesting season. Return the way you came.

2.0 Arrive back at the trailhead.

Options

To explore more of Schooner Head Path, instead of turning left on Murphy Lane, continue straight (north) on the well-graded path as it parallels Schooner Head Road. In another .5 mile you reach a junction with the Orange & Black Path on the left (west), a more difficult trail that leads up Champlain's east face and connects to the Champlain North Ridge and Precipice Trails. Beyond that junction, Schooner Head Path continues another 1.6 miles northwest and then north to northeast all the way to Compass Harbor on the outskirts of Bar Harbor. Some parts of the northern section of Schooner Head Path cross private property, so be respectful of property owners' rights and stay on the established route.

8 Sand Beach and Great Head Trail

Enjoy Acadia's only sandy ocean beach, made of sand, tiny shell fragments, quartz, and pink feldspar. Sand Beach is one of the few cold water, shell-based sand beaches in the world—a geological rarity, according to the National Park Service. Then take a hike along the Great Head Trail for its expansive views of the Beehive, Champlain Mountain, Otter Cliff, Egg Rock, and the Cranberry Isles. Also visible just off the tip of Great Head peninsula is an unusual rock formation called Old Soaker.

Distance: 1.7-mile lollipop
Hiking time: 1 to 1.5 hours
Difficulty: Moderate
Trail surface: Beach, rock ledges, forest floor
Best season: Spring through fall, particularly early morning or late afternoon in summer to avoid the beach crowds
Other trail users: Sunbathers on Sand Beach in summertime
Canine compatibility: Dogs prohibited on Sand Beach from June 15 through the weekend after Labor Day; leashed dogs permitted other times of year
Nat Geo Trails Illustrated Topographic Map: Acadia National Park
Special considerations: Seasonal restrooms and changing area are available at the Sand Beach parking lot; bring extra socks or a towel in case your feet get wet if you need to cross a small channel to get from the beach to the trailhead.

Finding the trailhead: From the park's visitor center, drive south on the Park Loop Road for about 3 miles; turn left (east) at the sign for Sand Beach. Follow the one-way Park Loop Road for about 5.5 miles past the park entrance station, to the beach parking lot on the left (east) side of the road. The Island Explorer stops at the beach parking lot. Walk down the stairs at the eastern end of the parking lot and head east across Sand Beach to the Great Head trailhead. GPS: N44 19.45' / W68 11.01'

The Hike

A hike on the Great Head peninsula is a perfect way to break up a lazy summer afternoon lounging on Sand Beach. Because it is so quintessentially Acadia, it's also a perfect place to bring first-time visitors, as we have with our nieces Sharon, Michelle, and Stacey.

Great Head is one of the highest headlands on the East Coast. A relatively modest scramble up the rocky slope of Great Head leads to dramatic views of the beach you just left behind, as well as vistas of such other notable park features as the Beehive, Champlain Mountain, and Otter Cliff.

Once, when we hiked Great Head with Sharon and Michelle, the views were made even more dramatic by the fog that first enveloped Sand Beach and the Beehive behind us and then receded like the outgoing tide.

"I feel like I'm living in a postcard," said Sharon, 15 at the time.

"This is really fun," said Michelle, 12 at the time, as opposed to the "kind of fun" rating she gave to a hike with less dramatic views the day before.

Since the 1840s and 1850s, Great Head has been a popular destination for artists and tourists. Thomas Cole, founder of the Hudson River School, hiked routes like Sand Beach and Great Head in 1842 and, along with fellow artists of his era, helped lay the groundwork for the current trail system on Mount Desert Island.

Great Head is steeped in Acadia history. A stone teahouse, known as Satterlee's Tower, once stood on the summit, and the ruins of it are still visible. It was built on the old estate of lawyer Herbert Satterlee and his wife, Louisa, the daughter of J. P. Morgan. The famous banker had given Great Head and Sand Beach to his daughter in 1910; his granddaughter, Eleanor, donated the land to Acadia two years after the great fire of 1947.

Once, as we stood by the teahouse ruins with Stacey, the ringing of a nearby buoy almost sounded like a clock tower chiming that it's time for tea. It was one of Stacey's first hikes in Acadia, and she was struck by the contrast of sand beach and rocky summit. "That's very rare," said Stacey.

From the parking lot, head down the stairs to the beach and walk 0.1 mile to the farthest (easternmost) end. You may need to cross a channel to the Great Head trailhead depending on the water level.

Go up a series of fifty-two granite steps bordered by split-rail fence. At the top of the steps, at 0.2 mile, turn right (southeast) and follow the blue blazes up the rocky ledge. Views of Sand Beach, the Beehive, and Champlain Mountain are immediately visible.

At the next trail junction, at about 0.3 mile, bear right (south) to head toward the tip of the peninsula, with views of Old Soaker, a nearby outcropping that appears rectangular at low tide, and of Otter Cliff and the Cranberry Isles in the distance.

At 0.6 mile the trail rounds the peninsula. At 0.9 mile reaches the summit of Great Head, where there are views Frenchman Bay and Egg Rock.

At about 1.2 miles, along a level section of the trail, you reach a junction in a birch grove. Turn left (southwest) at

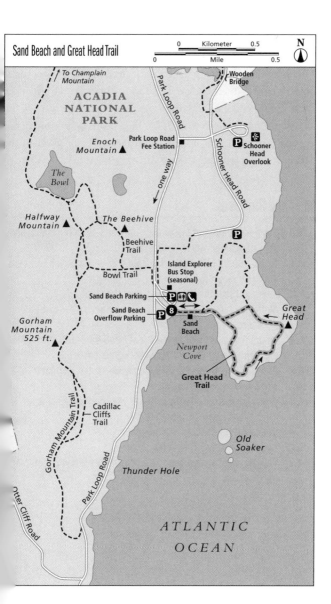

Sand Beach and Great Head Trail

N

Kilometer
0   0.5

Mile
0   0.5

To Champlain
Mountain

**ACADIA
NATIONAL
PARK**

Enoch
Mountain ▲

Park Loop Road
Fee Station

Park Loop Road

Wooden
Bridge

P Schooner
Head
Overlook

Schooner Head Road

The
Bowl

Halfway
Mountain ▲

The Beehive ▲

Beehive
Trail

one way

Bowl Trail

P

Island Explorer
Bus Stop
(seasonal)

Sand Beach Parking **P** 🚻 📞

Sand Beach
Overflow Parking **P 8**

Sand
Beach

Great
Head ▲

Gorham
Mountain
525 ft. ▲

Newport
Cove

**Great Head
Trail**

Gorham Mountain Trail

Cadillac
Cliffs
Trail

Park Loop Road

Otter Cliff Road

Thunder Hole

Old
Soaker

**ATLANTIC
OCEAN**

ascend gradually up the rocky spine of Great Head ridge, with views of Champlain Mountain, the Beehive, and Gorham Mountain. (If you go straight, northwest, at this junction to a parking lot near Schooner Head Road and then circle back, you can add another 0.8 mile to the loop.)

At the last junction, at 1.4 miles, bear right (northwest) to return to the trailhead and Sand Beach. Head back to the parking lot for a lollipop-loop hike of 1.7 miles.

Miles and Directions

0.0 Start at the edge of the parking lot, head down the stairs, and walk east along Sand Beach.

0.1 Cross a small channel at the east end of the beach to reach the Great Head trailhead.

0.2 Bear right (southeast) at the top of the stairs.

0.3 At the junction with the spur trail inland, go right (south) along the shore.

0.4 Reach the south end of the Great Head peninsula and follow the trail as it curves northeast along the shore.

0.9 Arrive at the Great Head summit, where the remnants of a stone teahouse can be found.

1.2 At the junction in the birch grove with the spur trail to Great Head ridge, bear left (southwest).

1.4 Bear right (northwest) at the junction.

1.6 Arrive back at the Great Head trailhead.

1.7 Walk west along the beach back to the parking lot, completing the loop.

9 Ocean Path

This easy hike takes you along Acadia's distinct pink-granite coastline, bringing you to Thunder Hole, where you may hear a reverberating boom as the surf crashes against a rocky chasm; Otter Cliff, where you may see rock climbers on the 60-foot precipice; and Otter Point, where you may catch a colorful sunset.

Distance: 4.6 miles out and back
Hiking time: 2 to 2.5 hours
Difficulty: Easy
Trail surface: Graded gravel path, forest floor
Best season: Spring through fall, particularly early morning or late afternoon in summer to avoid the crowds
Other trail users: Motorists stopping along the Park Loop Road to view Thunder Hole or Otter Point, rock climbers accessing Otter Cliff
Canine compatibility: Leashed dogs permitted

Nat Geo Trails Illustrated Topographic Map: Acadia National Park
Special considerations: Seasonal restrooms available at Sand Beach parking lot; restrooms at Thunder Hole (seasonal) and Fabbri (year-round) parking areas. A short part of Ocean Path that includes a viewing platform is accessible for visitors with wheelchairs or baby strollers, across from the first parking lot on the right, 0.3 mile south of Sand Beach.

Finding the trailhead: From the park's visitor center, drive south on the Park Loop Road for about 3 miles and turn left (east) at the sign for Sand Beach. Follow the one-way Park Loop Road for about 5.5 miles, past the park entrance station, to the beach parking lot on the left (east) side of the road. The trailhead is on the right (east) just before the stairs to the beach. The Island Explorer stops at the beach parking lot. GPS: N44 19.45' / W68 11.01'

The Hike

The sounds of the ocean and the views of rocky cliffs and pink-granite shoreline are never far from Ocean Path. At Thunder Hole, halfway along the path, when the conditions are just right, the surf crashes through rocky chasms with a thunderous roar. And at Otter Point, at trail's end, the sound of a buoy ringing fills the air. Rock climbers can be seen scaling Otter Cliff, one of the premier rock climbing areas in the eastern United States, while picnickers, birders, and sun worshippers can be found enjoying themselves on the flat pink-granite slabs that dot the shore here.

First used as a buckboard road in the 1870s, Ocean Path and Ocean Drive were incorporated into John D. Rockefeller Jr.'s vision of scenic roads, bringing visitors to many of Mount Desert Island's unique features. He began motor-road construction in the park in 1927 and hired landscape architect Frederick Law Olmsted Jr. to lay out many of the routes, including the Otter Cliff section of Ocean Drive. Ocean Path, first described in 1874, was substantially reconstructed by the Civilian Conservation Corps during the 1930s' Great Depression, with funding assistance from Rockefeller.

Because of its ease and accessibility, Ocean Path can be crowded during the height of the tourist season. The best time to walk it is either very early or very late on a summer's day, or in the spring or fall. If you explore the shore along Ocean Path, park officials ask that you please stay on designated routes to and from the path.

Ocean Path, often battered by storms and worn from heavy use, was extensively rehabilitated by the Acadia trail crew during the past decade. Some major repairs were needed again after the path was seriously damaged in early January 2024 rainstorms that ravaged the Maine coast.

The Ocean Path trailhead is on the right just before the stairs to Sand Beach. Follow the gravel path past the changing rooms and restrooms, up a series of stairs, and then left (south) away from a secondary parking area. The easy trail takes you southwest along the shore, paralleling the Ocean Drive section of the Park Loop Road.

Thunder Hole, a popular destination, is at 1.0 mile. Many visitors driving through the park on calm summer days stop here, causing a traffic jam, but go away disappointed. It turns out the best time to experience the power of Thunder Hole is after a storm and as high tide approaches, when the surf crashes violently through the chasms, pushing trapped air against the rock and creating a sound like the clap of thunder.

But even when you know the best time to hear Thunder Hole live up to its name, it can still take a number of times before you hit it right. On one trip to Acadia, we went with our nieces Sharon and Michelle to this spot three times, once late at night with stormy seas, but didn't hear the thundering boom as we expected.

If you visit Thunder Hole during stormy conditions, be careful. Visitors have been swept out to sea here and at Schoodic Point—a reminder of how powerful nature can be along Acadia's coast. Watch out for large waves, stay a safe distance away, and don't turn your back on the ocean.

At 1.3 miles on Ocean Path, you pass a short series of stairs on the right (west), which lead across the Park Loop Road to the Gorham Mountain trailhead. Monument Cove, with its bold pink granite column, is near this trailhead.

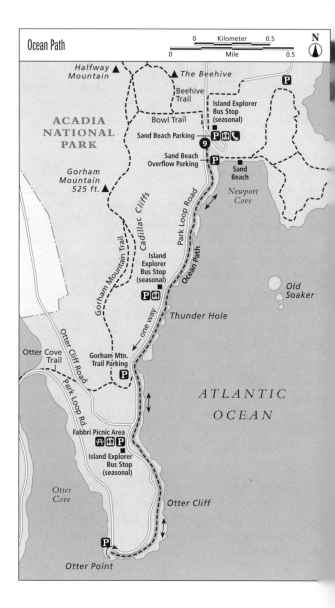

Ocean Path

| 0 | Kilometer | 0.5 |
| 0 | Mile | 0.5 |

N

Halfway Mountain

▲ *The Beehive*

Beehive Trail

ACADIA NATIONAL PARK

Bowl Trail

Island Explorer Bus Stop (seasonal)

Sand Beach Parking

9

Sand Beach Overflow Parking

Gorham Mountain 525 ft. ▲

Cadillac Cliffs

Gorham Mountain Trail

Park Loop Road

Ocean Path

Island Explorer Bus Stop (seasonal)

Sand Beach

Newport Cove

Old Soaker

Thunder Hole

one way

Gorham Mtn. Trail Parking

ATLANTIC OCEAN

Otter Cliff Road

Otter Cove Trail

Park Loop Rd.

Fabbri Picnic Area

Island Explorer Bus Stop (seasonal)

Otter Cove

Otter Cliff

Otter Point

The path's only noticeable elevation gain comes as it ~~~ses through the woods toward Otter Cliff, reached at 1.8 ~~iles. On the approach, you can see rock climbers scaling ~~e rock face or waiting at the top of the cliffs for their turn. ~~ staircase leads down on the left (east) to the rock climbers' ~~gistration board.

Ocean Path ends at 2.3 miles, at Otter Point, where you ~~n watch the sun set over Acadia and find a nearby com-~~emorative plaque dedicated to Rockefeller. A new bronze ~~aque, financed by contributions to replace the 1960s ~~iginal, was dedicated in 2016 during a ceremony attended ~~ about twenty Rockefeller family members, including the ~~ungest of Rockefeller's six children, banker and conser-~~tionist David Rockefeller Sr., who died in 2017 at the age ~~ 101.

Return the way you came.

~~es and Directions

~~.0 Start at the Ocean Path trailhead, on the right just before the stairs to Sand Beach. Follow the gravel path up a series of stairs and then left (south) away from a secondary parking area.

~~.0 Reach Thunder Hole (a viewing platform there may be closed during stormy seas).

~~.3 Pass the Gorham Mountain trailhead, which is across the Park Loop Road.

~~.8 Reach Otter Cliff, where you can see rock climbers scaling the precipice.

~~.3 Arrive at Otter Point, where you can watch the sun set. Return the way you came.

~~6 Arrive back at the trailhead.

10 The Bowl Trail

This hike leads to a mountain pond called the Bowl, wher
you can encounter wildlife, especially if you travel early i
the morning or late in the afternoon. You can connect t
the Gorham Mountain and Champlain South Ridge Trai
off this trail. And you can find more moderate ascents up th
back side of the nearby Beehive, a nice alternative to clim
ing the iron ladder rungs up that peak's cliff.

Distance: 1.6 miles out and back
Hiking time: 1.5 to 2 hours
Difficulty: Moderate
Trail surface: Forest floor, rock
ledges
Best season: Spring through fall,
particularly early morning or late
afternoon in summer to avoid the
crowds
Other trail users: Hikers climbing
the Beehive

Canine compatibility: Leashed
dogs permitted (but not on the
ladder climb up the Beehive)
**Nat Geo Trails Illustrated
Topographic Map:** Acadia
National Park
Special considerations:
Seasonal restrooms at Sand
Beach parking lot

Finding the trailhead: From the park's visitor center, drive south on
the Park Loop Road for about 3 miles and turn left (east) at the sig
for Sand Beach. Follow the one-way Park Loop Road for about 5.5
miles, past the park entrance station, to the beach parking lot on th
left (east) side of the road. The Island Explorer stops at the beach
parking lot. Follow the pedestrian crosswalk to the other side of the
Park Loop Road to reach the trailhead, diagonally (northwest) acros
from the beach parking lot. GPS: N44 19.54' / W68 11.07'

iews of a great blue heron taking off low across the water's
urface or of a turkey vulture soaring high on the thermals
e among the possible rewards when you hike to the Bowl,
mountain pond at more than 400 feet in elevation.

We were lucky and got both views in the same day
we hiked along the shoreline. Another time, during a
alk down from the Bowl, we heard a loud snorting in the
oods. A couple of white-tailed deer darted through the
es, the snorting apparently an alarm call. Another day, on
e way off an early-morning Beehive climb, we were sur-
sed by a large barred owl staring silently down at us from a
e. Hike in the early morning or late afternoon to improve
ur chances of such wildlife encounters.

The Bowl lies between Champlain Mountain and the
ehive, and it also occupies a special spot in Acadia history.
1908, Eliza Homans, a longtime Bar Harbor resident,
ated the first large section of land, which included the
wl and the Beehive, to an organization seeking to create
park, setting the stage for more big land donations to
ow.

The Bowl Trail begins by climbing gradually through a
land birch forest, passing a junction with the very steep
hive Trail, featuring iron ladder rungs, at 0.2 mile.

A spur to the Gorham Mountain Trail is at 0.4 mile;
ther spur to the Beehive, a more gradual alternative to
ladder approach, is at 0.5 mile, at the same place where
Gorham Mountain Trail comes in.

3eyond, the Bowl Trail heads up steeply through the
ds and then goes downhill, arriving at the Bowl at the
mile mark. Champlain Mountain, the seventh-highest

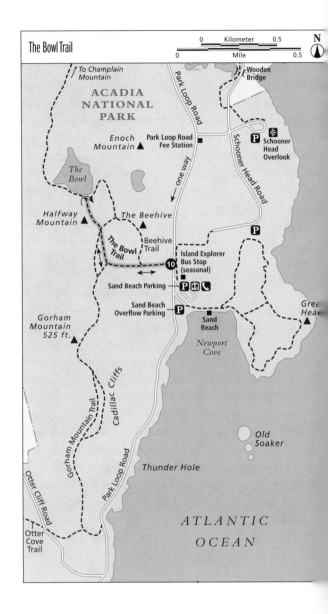

The Bowl Trail

| 0 | Kilometer | 0.5 |
| 0 | Mile | 0.5 |

N

To Champlain
Mountain

ACADIA
NATIONAL
PARK

Wooden
Bridge

Enoch
Mountain ▲

Park Loop Road
Fee Station

Park Loop Road

Schooner Head Road

P Schooner
Head
Overlook

The
Bowl

one way

Halfway
Mountain ▲

The Beehive

The Bowl
Trail

Beehive
Trail

P

10

Island Explorer
Bus Stop
(seasonal)

Sand Beach Parking

P

Sand Beach
Overflow Parking

P

Sand
Beach

Great
Head ▲

Gorham
Mountain
525 ft. ▲

Newport
Cove

Gorham Mountain Trail

Cadillac Cliffs

Park Loop Road

Otter Cliff Road

Thunder Hole

Old
Soaker

Otter
Cove
Trail

ATLANTIC
OCEAN

peak in Acadia, overlooks the Bowl to the north, while trail-
ess Enoch Mountain is to the northeast (right).

This also marks the junction with the 1.6-mile Champlain South Ridge Trail, which heads left (northwest), and
another moderate spur to the Beehive, which heads right
east).

Return the way you came.

Miles and Directions

0.0 Start at the Bowl trailhead, diagonally (northwest) across the
Park Loop Road from the Sand Beach parking lot.

0.2 Reach the junction with the Beehive Trail, a very steep ladder
climb that heads right, up that peak's cliff.

0.4 A spur trail to the Gorham Mountain Trail heads left at this
junction.

0.5 A more moderate spur trail up the Beehive heads right at this
junction. The Gorham Mountain Trail heads left here.

0.8 Arrive at the Bowl and the junction with the Champlain South
Ridge Trail and another moderate spur trail up the Beehive.
Return the way you came.

1.6 Arrive back at the trailhead.

11 Gorham Mountain Trail

This is a classic Acadia hike to a 525-foot peak with sweeping views of Great Head, Sand Beach, Otter Cliff, Champlain Mountain, and the Beehive. The trail, among the most traveled in the park, is also one of the most historic, dating back to the early 1900s and the Great Depression. The hike includes a spur trail to Cadillac Cliffs and an ancient sea cave.

Distance: 1.8 miles out and back
Hiking time: 1 to 1.5 hours
Difficulty: Moderate
Trail surface: Forest floor, rock ledges, rock steps
Best season: Spring through fall, particularly early morning or late afternoon in summer to avoid the crowds
Other trail users: Campers at Blackwoods Campground hiking up Gorham via the Quarry and Otter Cove Trails

Canine compatibility: Leashed dogs permitted (but not recommended on the optional Cadillac Cliffs Trail, which features a couple of iron rungs)
Nat Geo Trails Illustrated Topographic Map: Acadia National Park
Special considerations: No facilities at trailhead, but nearby restrooms at Thunder Hole (seasonal) and Fabbri (year-round) parking areas

Finding the trailhead: From the park's visitor center, drive south on the Park Loop Road for about 3 miles and turn left (east) at the sign for Sand Beach. Follow the one-way Park Loop Road for about 7 miles, passing the park entrance station, Sand Beach, and Thunder Hole, to the Gorham Mountain sign and parking lot on the right (west) side of the road. The Island Explorer does not have a stop here, but you may be able to ask the bus driver to let you off if it is safe to do so. GPS: N44 19.00' / W68 11.28'

The Hike

Charlie Jacobi, a retired ranger at Acadia National Park, estimates that he's hiked the Gorham Mountain Trail maybe 00 times over the years, mostly as part of the job. But he ys it never gets old.

"Every day is different," said Jacobi during a recent hike n a sunny afternoon to the peak of Gorham, noted for me of the most rewarding views in Acadia.

The trail is among the most popular in the park, and it's sy to see why.

"This whole ridge—Gorham, Champlain, and the Bee-ve—is close to the ocean," says Jacobi, who retired in 2017 er working thirty-three years at the park. "You're right on p of it—almost. That's what makes it attractive."

The trail, marked by historic-style cairns that Jacobi lped reintroduce to the park, follows the great ridge that ns all the way to Champlain Mountain and is the closest the ocean of all of Acadia's mountain ridges.

An additional bonus, if you choose to take it, is the 0.5-le spur trail to the once-submerged Cadillac Cliffs and ancient sea cave, which illustrates the powerful geologic ces that helped shape Mount Desert Island.

From the parking lot, bypass the Otter Cove Trail that nnects to Blackwoods Campground and comes in on the (southwest) near the trailhead. Bear right on the Gorham untain Trail to climb gradually through an evergreen st and up open ledges, heading north. Though the trail ften shaded by conifers in this section, the sounds of the an surf signal that the shore is nearby.

At 0.2 mile the Cadillac Cliffs Trail leads right (north-), paralleling and then rejoining the Gorham Mountain

Trail at 0.5 mile. (If you want to add the Cadillac Cliff spur, it is best to do it on the ascent rather than the descent because of the iron rungs and steep rock face along the way.) Don't miss a bronze memorial at this intersection honoring Waldron Bates, chair of the Roads and Paths Committee of the Bar Harbor Village Improvement Association from 1900 to 1909, who developed the century-old style of cairn now used to mark many Acadia trails.

Stay on the Gorham Mountain Trail and ascend moderately; a near-barren island called Old Soaker comes into sight through the trees.

All along this portion of the route you will enjoy views south to Otter Cliff, northeast to Great Head and Sand Beach, and north to the Beehive and Champlain Mountain. Frenchman Bay and Egg Rock can be seen in the distance to the east.

We stop when we spot a Bates-style cairn in need of repair.

In 2002, Jacobi and Gary Stellpflug, then foreman of the Acadia trails crew, revived the use of the Bates-style cairn, which consist of two to four base stones with a lintel laid across them, capped by a pointer stone.

The Gorham Mountain Trail is home to many of the eponymous cairns and was part of a research study Jacobi led to test the effectiveness of signs in discouraging people from stacking stone, dismantling, or otherwise damaging cairns. As one sign near a cairn cautioned, adding or removing rocks misleads hikers, causes erosion, and kills plants and degrades the mountain landscape.

We reach the peak of Gorham Mountain at 0.9 mile. At the 525-foot summit, looking northeast, Jacobi points to the back side of the Beehive.

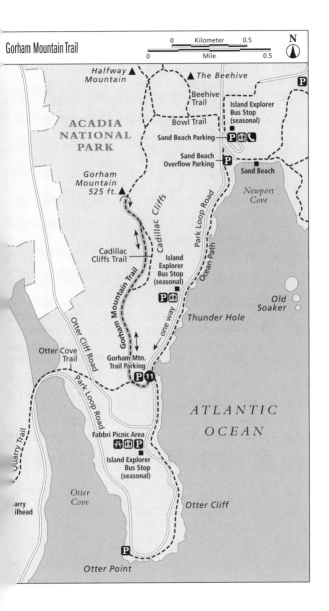

Gorham Mountain Trail

Kilometer 0 0.5
Mile 0 0.5

N

Halfway Mountain ▲   ▲ *The Beehive*

Beehive Trail

Bowl Trail

ACADIA NATIONAL PARK

Island Explorer Bus Stop (seasonal)

Sand Beach Parking 🅿🚻📞

Sand Beach Overflow Parking 🅿

🅿

Sand Beach ■

Gorham Mountain 525 ft. ▲

Cadillac Cliffs

Newport Cove

Cadillac Cliffs Trail

Park Loop Road

Island Explorer Bus Stop (seasonal)

🅿🚻

Gorham Mountain Trail

Ocean Path

one way

Old Soaker

Thunder Hole

Otter Cove Trail

Gorham Mtn. Trail Parking

🅿 **11**

Otter Cliff Road

Park Loop Road

ATLANTIC OCEAN

Quarry Trail

Fabbri Picnic Area 🏕🚻🅿

Island Explorer Bus Stop (seasonal)

arry ilhead

Otter Cove

Otter Cliff

🅿

Otter Point

To the north, a small hill called Halfway Mountain is situated below Champlain Mountain and Huguenot Head; to the west are Dorr and Cadillac Mountains.

On the mainland in the distance is Schoodic Mountain with its radio tower, and then the Schoodic Peninsula to the east. The Cranberry Islands, including Baker Island and its 1855 light tower, are to the south.

Return the way you came.

On the trek down, listen for the sounds of a bell buoy located near an ocean ledge. On a day when the sky is blue and the sun bright, the ocean can appear almost tropical.

"Oh my God," said Jacobi. "This is spectacular."

No matter how many times you hike the Gorham Mountain Trail, it's always rewarding.

Miles and Directions

0.0 Start at the Gorham Mountain trailhead, which leaves from a parking lot on the right (west) side of the one-way Park Loop Road. Coming in on the left just after the trailhead is the Otter Cove Trail that links to Blackwoods Campground. Bear right at the junction to continue on the Gorham Mountain Trail.

0.2 Reach the junction with the southern end of the Cadillac Cliff Trail. Stay straight to continue on Gorham Mountain Trail.

0.5 Pass the junction with the northern end of the Cadillac Cliff Trail, which comes in from the right (east).

0.9 Arrive on the Gorham Mountain summit. Return the way you came.

1.8 Arrive back at the trailhead.

12 Jordan Pond Path

This hike offers expansive views of Jordan Pond, the Bubbles, and Jordan Cliffs, as well as a chance to glimpse a colorful merganser duck or busy beaver or watch kayakers plying the waters. The graded gravel path on the east side of the pond is particularly easy, and an amazing 4,000 feet of log bridges on the west side helps smooth the way over what would otherwise be a potentially wet, rocky, and rooted trail.

Distance: 3.3-mile loop

Hiking time: 1.5 to 2 hours

Difficulty: Easy

Trail surface: Graded gravel path, rock slabs, forest floor, log bridges, log boardwalk

Best season: Spring through fall, particularly early morning or late afternoon in summer to avoid the crowds

Other trail users: Motorists using Jordan Pond boat ramp road that crosses the trail to unload their canoes or kayaks, people taking their bikes to the nearby Jordan Pond House

Canine compatibility: Leashed dogs permitted on the trail but not in Jordan Pond

Nat Geo Trails Illustrated Topographic Map: Acadia National Park

Special considerations: Certain sections of the graded gravel path on the east, west, and south sides of pond are accessible to wheelchairs and baby strollers. It's important to arrive early in the morning or late in the afternoon during the busy season to find a parking spot. There is a chemical toilet at the trailhead; full facilities are available seasonally at nearby Jordan Pond House.

Finding the trailhead: From the park's visitor center, head south on Park Loop Road for about 7.6 miles and turn right (north) into the

Jordan Pond north lot. Park in the lot on the right. Follow the boat ram
road down to the shore of the pond. The trailhead is on the right (eas
and leads around the pond. The Island Explorer stops at the nearby
Jordan Pond House. GPS: N44 19.22' / W68 15.13'

The Hike

A vigorous walk around Jordan Pond, capped by afternoo
tea and popovers on the lawn of the Jordan Pond House-
it's one of those special Acadia experiences.

The trail starts from the end of the boat ramp road
the Jordan Pond north parking lot and immediately off
a spectacular view of the rounded mountains known as t
Bubbles, which lie north across the pond. Bear right (eas
circling the pond counterclockwise.

The first half of the trail is along the easy eastern sho
with its graded gravel path, but be prepared for the weste
shore's rock slabs and long series of log bridges known a
bogwalk. The rocks and log bridges can be slippery wh
wet. Wear proper footwear.

At 0.2 mile you reach the first of several trails t
diverge from the Jordan Pond Path. Bear left, parallel
the shore at each of the junctions. The trail rounds a be
at the southeasterly end of the pond, across a rock path t
was originally built in the early 1900s, providing pond
wetlands views.

At 0.3 mile pass the junction with the Bubble & Jor
Ponds Path (formerly known as the Pond Trail), which le
to trails up Pemetic Mountain. Stay on Jordan Pond P
along the eastern shore of the pond.

The trail now begins heading north. You soon start see
Jordan Cliffs to the west across the pond. There are plent

oulders along the shore to sit on and admire the crystal-clear
aters and the tremendous views. At 150 feet, Jordan Pond is
e deepest lake in Acadia and the fifth largest, behind Echo
ake, Seal Cove Pond, Eagle Lake, and Long Pond. Jordan
ond also serves as a public water supply, so no swimming or
en putting a foot in the water is allowed.

After passing over a series of wooden bridges, you soon
me up under the towering pinkish granite of South Bub-
e near the north side of the pond.

At 1.1 miles you reach Jordan Pond Carry and the Bubbles
ail (South Bubble Trail), which veer to the right (north) and
d, respectively, to Eagle Lake and South Bubble.

At 1.6 miles pass the junction with Bubbles Divide, a trail
at heads right (northeast) up the gap between North and
uth Bubbles and allows access to the precariously perched
bble Rock, which is visible from the Park Loop Road.
u are now at the northernmost end of the pond and can
good views of the Jordan Pond House to the south and
Bubbles to the east. Cross a series of intricate wooden
dges—one rustic-style span has an archway in the middle.

At 1.7 miles pass the junction with the Deer Brook Trail,
ich leads up toward Penobscot Mountain and provides
ess to the Jordan Cliffs Trail and the beautiful double-
h Deer Brook Bridge, built in 1925 as part of the carriage
d system. The Deer Brook Trail was the setting for a
ne in the movie of Stephen King's *Pet Sematary*.

Now begins the trail's traverse of the rougher western
re of the pond, with its rock slabs and long series of log
lges. After a bit of hide-and-seek with the shore and a
tch of rock hopping, you reach the log bridges that take
over fragile wetlands.

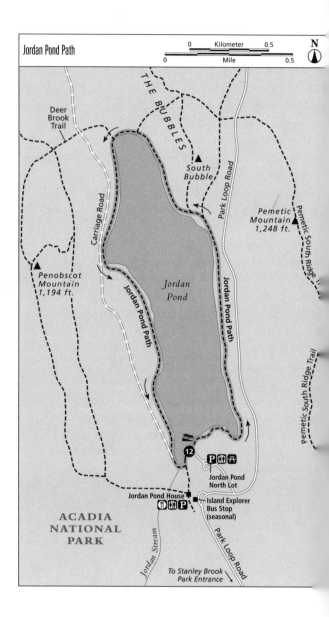

Jordan Pond Path

THE BUBBLES

Deer Brook Trail

South Bubble

Carriage Road

Penobscot Mountain 1,194 ft.

Pemetic Mountain 1,248 ft.

Pemetic South Ridge Trail

Jordan Pond

Jordan Pond Path

Jordan Pond Path

Pemetic South Ridge Trail

12

Jordan Pond North Lot

Jordan Pond House

Island Explorer Bus Stop (seasonal)

ACADIA NATIONAL PARK

Jordan Stream

Park Loop Road

Park Loop Road

To Stanley Brook Park Entrance

0   Kilometer   0.5
0   Mile   0.5

N

A project to replace the bogwalk on the west shore was completed in 2020 after four seasons of work, mostly by friends of Acadia volunteers with support from the Acadia trails crew. Used mainly to protect wet or eroded trails in flat areas near ponds, bogwalks were introduced to Acadia in the early 1980s by now-retired trails foreman Gary Stellpflug.

In addition to the dramatic views of the Bubbles, you may catch a glimpse of a common merganser, as we did. It hard to miss a merganser, especially a female, with its rust-colored, crested head and orange bill. Evidence of beaver activity dots the shore of Jordan Pond; you may also see a beaver chowing down, as we have.

At 3.2 miles turn left onto the carriage road and cross a carriage road bridge. Then turn left again to follow the trail it circles back to the Jordan Pond north lot at 3.3 miles. st before you get back to the lot, you can turn right (south) d head up the hill to the Jordan Pond House for an Acadia dition of afternoon tea and popovers, with a grand view of e pond and the Bubbles as nature's backdrop.

les and Directions

0.0 Start at the Jordan Pond Path trailhead. At the end of the boat ramp road, turn right along the graded gravel path.

.2 Bear left at a junction and continue straight along the eastern shore of the pond.

.3 Reach the junction with the Bubble & Jordan Ponds Path (Pond Trail) and continue straight along the eastern shore of the pond.

.1 Reach the junction with Jordan Pond Carry and the Bubbles Trail (South Bubble Trail); continue straight along the eastern shore of the pond.

1.6 Reach the junction with Bubbles Divide, which goes northeast through the gap between North and South Bubbles. Continue along the shore as the path rounds the north side of the pond.

1.7 Reach the junction with the Deer Brook Trail, which leads up Penobscot Mountain. Continue along the shore of the pond, with the path now following the west side.

3.2 Turn left onto the carriage road and cross a carriage road bridge, and then turn left again to follow the path as it circles back to the Jordan Pond north lot.

3.3 Arrive back at the trailhead, completing the loop.

13 Jordan Stream Path

It's a crisp woods walk from the Jordan Pond House along the meandering Jordan Stream to the main highlight of this trail: a carriage road bridge faced with cobblestones rather than the granite that surfaces other bridges in the carriage road system. Once badly eroded, this path benefits from a recent rehabilitation that includes patio-style stone steps along the shore, rebuilt wooden bridges, and new bogwalk.

Distance: 1.2 miles out and back
Hiking time: 30 minutes to 1 hour
Difficulty: Easy to moderate
Trail surface: Wooden bridges, stone steps, forest floor
Best season: Spring through fall
Other trail users: Passengers getting off a horse-drawn carriage to view Cobblestone Bridge

Canine compatibility: Leashed dogs permitted
Nat Geo Trails Illustrated Topographic Map: Acadia National Park
Special considerations: Full seasonal facilities at the Jordan Pond House

Finding the trailhead: From the park's visitor center, drive south on the Park Loop Road for about 7.6 miles and turn right (north) into the Jordan Pond north lot. Park in the lot on the left (south) and follow signs to the Jordan Pond House. Walk past the Jordan Pond House, turn right (west) to head behind the building, and follow a path marked "To Asticou, Spring Trail, Penobscot & Sargent Mtn Trails" down to a carriage road. The trailhead is across the carriage road on the left. The Island Explorer stops at the Jordan Pond House. GPS: N44 19.13' W68 15.19'

The Hike

Jordan Stream Path is among the shortest and easiest hikes in Acadia National Park, but it ends at one of the park's most unusual and historic landmarks: Cobblestone Bridge.

Previously worn and overrun with roots, the path benefited from extensive rehabilitation in 2015 overseen by Christian Barter, a park trail crew supervisor who is also the park's poet laureate. The work included rebuilding four wooden bridges, totaling 59 feet; rerouting 300 feet of the path higher and farther from the stream; and adding about 400 feet of bogwalk (or wide double planks close to the ground), a patio-style stone walkway next to the stream, and new signs and drainage systems.

Jordan Stream, a habitat for sea-run brook trout, seems like something out of a Robert Frost poem, with small waterfalls, pools, and rushing water in season. The stream starts at the south end of Jordan Pond and goes all the way to Little Long Pond near Seal Harbor.

The path was part of a pre-1760 Native American carry trail and was built in 1902 by the Seal Harbor Village Improvement Association as a scenic connector between the village and Jordan Pond, according to the National Park Service report on the Mount Desert Island Hiking Trail System.

The path starts near the busy Jordan Pond House, but is often overlooked by hikers who opt for more prominent hikes in the area.

Jim Linnane, a volunteer with the Friends of Acadia whose volunteers helped in the path rehabilitation, notes that thick spruce forests—untouched by the great fire of 1947—help keep the path often private and quiet.

"Hiking the Jordan Stream trail, I often think about how special it is, especially because it is so close to the mass of humanity that descends on the Jordan Pond area on a nice day," Linnane said. "Surprisingly, even after a very dry summer, the Jordan Stream still has some running water. The gurgle and trickle of the stream is a welcome and wonderful interruption to the silence of the deep woods."

While it is often a pleasant gurgle in late summer, Jordan Stream can become a torrent after a rainstorm, with cascades and rapids rushing and tumbling beside the path. It can be a spectacular show, but high water often submerges sections of the trail and wears it down.

The path is within park boundaries for about 0.5 mile, but just outside the park it reaches the famed Cobblestone Bridge, the only span in the carriage road system faced with naturally rounded cobblestones. The other bridges are surfaced with granite.

The 150-foot-long, 21-foot-high bridge was built in 1917 and was the first major structure constructed as part of the carriage road system on Mount Desert Island, according to *Acadia's Carriage Roads* by Robert A. Thayer.

Sixteen of the seventeen bridges were paid for by John D. Rockefeller Jr., the only son of the founder of a giant oil company; the last was financed by the park in 1941. Rockefeller came up with the idea for the carriage roads and oversaw details of construction starting in 1913, with 45 miles currently within the park boundaries.

While the hike's destination, the Cobblestone Bridge, is much photographed now, it may not always have been so well loved.

According to *Rockefeller Carriage Roads*, a Historic American Engineering Record report that stems from research administered by the National Park Service from 1994 to 1995, George B. Dorr, Acadia's first park superintendent, criticized the bridge's construction in a 1924 letter to NPS assistant director Arno B. Cammerer, writing that "all have agreed in regretting it from the artistic standpoint," but it would soon be "little noticeable" because vegetation was closing around it.

The report says Rockefeller had planned for a granite-faced bridge, but his engineer, Charles Simpson, instead urged the use of native cobbles, or rounded stones, from the streambed.

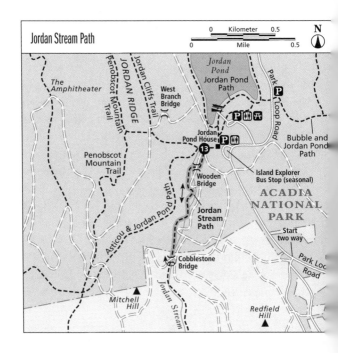

Jordan Stream Path itself is easy to reach, with the trailhead located at the carriage road behind the Jordan Pond House.

Follow the narrow path through the woods, paralleling the stream as it tumbles south toward the ocean. Part of the trail features more than thirty neatly laid stepping stones, making it seem like a garden path at times.

When you reach a junction with a carriage road at 0.2 mile, bear right (west) across a wooden bridge. Pick up the trail at the end of the bridge, heading left (south) down the other side of the stream.

The trail descends, and a series of wooden footbridges takes you across stream tributaries.

At 0.6 mile the trail brings you to the base of the Cobblestone Bridge. The trail continues toward Seal Harbor across private land, making the bridge a natural turnaround point.

Return the way you came.

Miles and Directions

0.0 Start at the Jordan Stream Path trailhead, across a carriage road behind the Jordan Pond House.

0.2 Reach a junction with a carriage road. Cross a wooden bridge to the right (west) and continue south down the trail along the western bank of Jordan Stream.

0.6 Reach Cobblestone Bridge. Return the way you came.

1.2 Arrive back at the trailhead.

14 Seaside Path

A newly rehabilitated historical gem, Seaside Path takes you under the Stanley Brook Bridge and by surrounding plantings designed by noted landscape architect Beatrix Farrand. Seaside Path starts near Jordan Pond and becomes seaside only when it reaches Seal Harbor Beach, open to the public and generously maintained by the Seal Harbor Village Improvement Society. Originally built about a century ago, the path fell into disuse and suffered from heavy water damage and erosion until rehabilitation was completed in 2020 after multiyear, collaborative effort led by the Acadia trails crew.

Distance: 4.0 miles out and back
Hiking time: 1 to 1.5 hours
Difficulty: Easy
Trail surface: Graded gravel path, forest floor
Best season: Spring through fall
Other trail users: Local residents, beachgoers
Canine compatibility: Leashed dogs permitted on path but prohibited on Seal Harbor Beach
Nat Geo Trails Illustrated Topographic Map: Acadia National Park

Special considerations: Full seasonal facilities at the Jordan Pond House and Seal Harbor Beach parking lot. Certain sections of the graded gravel path at the start near Jordan Pond House are accessible to visitors with wheelchairs or baby strollers. No lifeguards at Seal Harbor Beach; no dogs and no rock picking off beach allowed. Stay on the path and respect private property.

Finding the trailhead: From the park's visitor center, drive south on the Park Loop Road for about 7.6 miles and turn right (north) into the Jordan Pond north lot. Park in the lot on the left (south) and follow signs to the Jordan Pond House. Take a short gravel path diagonally opposite the main entrance of the Jordan Pond House and Island Explorer bus stop, following it past a bike rack on the eastern edge of the Jordan Pond House parking lot to a carriage road. Turn right (west) on the carriage road and take a quick left (south) onto Seaside Path. The Island Explorer stops at Jordan Pond House and at Seal Harbor Beach. GPS: N44 19.12' / W68 15.12'

The Hike

Seaside Path is a special trek in Acadia National Park. A stroll on the shady path is like stepping back in time after it was recently rehabilitated to look much as it did one hundred years ago. And it allows you to imagine what it must have been like to be able to stay at the former Seaside Inn and stroll over to the Jordan Pond House for afternoon tea and popovers.

The 2.0-mile hike through a mixed, mature forest takes you from the rounded mountains and steep cliffs of the Jordan Pond area to a sandy beach on Seal Harbor, one of only two public sandy ocean beaches on Mount Desert Island, the other being Acadia's Sand Beach.

There are no expansive views directly on the path, but it a "beautiful example" of a late 1800s to early 1900s gravel path, said Gary Stellpflug, now-retired foreman of the Acadia National Park trails crew. While it was a long haul to complete the rehabilitation, the final product is exquisite and reflects the historic period, he wrote in his annual report on Acadia's trails for 2020.

Access the start of Seaside Path from a short gravel path kitty-corner from the main entrance of the Jordan Pond House, following it past a bike rack to a carriage road in 0.1 mile. Turn right (west) on the carriage road and then take a quick left (south) to head down Seaside.

At 0.5 mile cross a carriage road, walk past some high pines, and reach the Stanley Brook Bridge at 0.8 mile. Here the path takes you under one of the side arches of the triple-arch bridge

Take some time to explore the bridge, which was completed in 1933, the last one to be designed and built by John D. Rockefeller Jr. It's one of Acadia's few carriage road bridges still featuring the original plantings designed by noted landscape architect Beatrix Farrand, as the great fire of 1947 destroyed much of her other work.

Acadia's seasonal two-lane Stanley Brook entrance road goes under the bridge's center arch; the other side arch spans Stanley Brook.

At 1.5 miles cross paved private Seaside Lane, remaining on the path to respect private property, and come to memorial for Edward Lothrop Rand. A Boston lawyer who was noted for coauthoring with botanist John Howard Redfield a late nineteenth-century book on the botany of Mount Desert Island, Rand also served as the first chairman of the Path Committee for the Seal Harbor Village Improvement Society, from 1900 to 1907.

At 1.7 miles reach private Seaside Lane again; turn right (south) and head slightly downhill as Seal Harbor comes into view.

Cross ME 3 at 1.9 miles and turn left along a sidewalk that overlooks granite and boulders at sandy Seal Harbor Beach's western end.

Look back across ME 3 and consider that the Seaside Inn once stood near the beach and was an institution Seal Harbor, owned by the same family for decades. While it thrived during the booming 1920s, a fantastic era yachts and summer travel, the inn became outdated and was demolished in 1964. In its heyday, visitors would come back each year to spend entire summers relaxing at the one-hundred-room inn, and many would walk Seaside Path to reach the Jordan Pond House, which offered its first popovers and tea in 1895.

As you walk along the sidewalk, you soon pass the park's Stanley Brook entrance and come to the thirty-one-space Seal Harbor Beach parking lot on the other side of ME 3. A pedestrian crosswalk allows you to safely cross over to use seasonal restrooms or catch the Island Explorer bus to your next destination if you decide not to retrace your steps to Jordan Pond House.

As you enjoy the views along Seal Harbor Beach, you can see why the area has been such a prime attraction over the years.

Seal Harbor was the summer home of John D. Rockefeller Jr., who co-founded Acadia National Park and financed construction of the park's 45 miles of carriage roads. His summer home, the ninety-nine-room Eyrie, was torn down, but his legacy remains. Rockefeller was deeply connected to the community of Seal Harbor in many ways.

Some of Rockefeller's secretaries stayed at the Seaside Inn during summers, and he would stop by at the end of each season to thank the bellhops, waiters, dishwashers, cooks, and other staff for their work, according to *Fond Memories of the Seaside Inn*, a compilation available through the Northeast Harbor Library.

Rockefeller donated the land for a public park and then worked with the Seal Harbor Village Improvement Society to demolish an old hotel and build a rolling village green that provides views of the beach. Landscaping legend Beatrix Farrand worked with the improvement society's path committee to create the lawn and small nearby park.

To this day the village green and beach benefit from generous care. Members of the village improvement society rake and clean the beach each morning, clean and maintain the comfort station and the parking lot, and provide comprehensive landscaping to keep the village green in top shape.

Rockefeller also purchased the Jordan Pond House in 1928 and gifted it to the National Park Service.

While the Seaside Inn on the southern end of Seaside Path was never rebuilt, the Jordan Pond House did rise again on the north end after the original building was destroyed by fire in 1979. A local nonprofit group raised money to construct the current building, and the restaurant reopened in 1982 to continue the tradition of the park's only restaurant.

As you return along Seaside Path to the Jordan Pond House, appreciate the hard work that went into rehabilitating the path, taking from 2017 to 2020. The work included building new culverts with historically accurate stone head walls, digging and compacting some areas that were once nearly impassable, and laying a new gravel surface atop a base of crushed stone along almost the entire length.

The extensive work on the path was a collaborative effort by the Acadia trails crew, volunteers with the Friends of Acadia, the Acadia Youth Conservation Corps, and contracted crew with the Appalachian Mountain Club, said Christian Barter, trails crew supervisor on the project.

In a video for the Friends of Acadia, Barter said about half of Seaside Path is on park land and almost another half of the trail goes through the nonprofit 1,400-acre Land & Garden Preserve, which includes lands added by the late David Rockefeller Sr., youngest child of John D. Rockefeller Jr., who died in 2017. A couple of private landowners also gave permission to restore portions of the trail through their property, Barter said.

The work on the trail was funded with donations to the nonprofit Friends of Acadia in 2016 during an annual fundraising benefit. In a traditional "paddle raise," sixty donors contributed a total of $318,000 to restore Seaside Path.

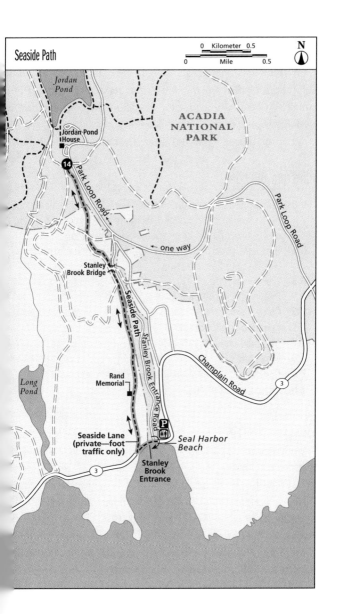

Seaside Path

0   Kilometer   0.5

0   Mile   0.5

N

Jordan
Pond

ACADIA
NATIONAL
PARK

Jordan Pond
House

14

Park Loop Road

Park Loop Road

← one way

Stanley
Brook Bridge

Seaside Path

Stanley Brook Entrance Road

Champlain Road

3

Rand
Memorial

Long
Pond

P

Seal Harbor
Beach

Seaside Lane
(private—foot
traffic only)

Stanley
Brook
Entrance

3

leading to the revival of an important link between two key areas for hikers on Mount Desert Island.

If you've worked up an appetite after the 4.0-mile round–trip hike and plan on tea and popovers at the Jordan Pond House, you can also appreciate the $356,000 rehabilitation of the famed tea lawn in 2018 while taking in the views across the pond of the distinctive twin mountains known as the Bubbles.

Miles and Directions

0.0 Start at a short gravel path kitty-corner from the main entrance of the Jordan Pond House and the Island Explorer bus stop, and follow it past a bike rack to a carriage road.

0.1 Turn right (west) on the carriage road and take a quick left (south) onto Seaside Path.

0.5 Cross a carriage road.

0.8 Reach Stanley Brook Bridge.

1.5 Cross paved private Seaside Lane and follow the path past a memorial for Edward Lothrop Rand.

1.7 Turn right (south) on Seaside Lane.

1.9 Cross ME 3 and turn left (east).

2.0 Reach Seal Harbor Beach. Return the way you came.

4.0 Arrive back at the trailhead.

Options

You can also start this trail at the Seal Harbor Beach parking lot, where there is parking for about thirty vehicles and season Island Explorer bus service. Parking and use of the beach a free. From the beach parking lot on ME 3, just to the east Acadia's seasonal Stanley Brook entrance, cross over to th sidewalk, turn right (west), and walk 0.1 mile to the priva Seaside Lane. Cross back over ME 3 and walk uphill (north) the private road (foot traffic only) and reach the start of Seasi Path at 0.3 mile, marked by a small sign on a tree on the l (west) by a red hydrant. Reach Jordan Pond House at 2.0 mil

15 Bubbles Divide

A moderate hike with some steep stretches brings you to 360-degree views from South Bubble and an up-close perspective of Bubble Rock, a precariously perched glacial erratic visible from the Park Loop Road that generations of hikers have playfully attempted to "push." From South Bubble, Jordan Pond and the Atlantic Ocean are to the south, Pemetic Mountain to the east, North Bubble to the north, and Sargent and Penobscot Mountains to the west.

Distance: 1.2 mile out and back
Hiking time: About 1 hour
Difficulty: Moderate to more challenging
Trail surface: Forest floor, rock ledges, log steps
Best season: Spring through fall, particularly early morning or late afternoon in summer to avoid the crowds
Other trail users: Hikers accessing North Bubble, Eagle Lake, or Jordan Pond

Canine compatibility: Leashed dogs permitted
Nat Geo Trails Illustrated Topographic Map: Acadia National Park
Special considerations: No facilities at trailhead; chemical toilet at Jordan Pond north lot and full seasonal facilities at Jordan Pond House, a short drive away. Very limited parking and no Island Explorer bus stop.

Finding the trailhead: From the park's visitor center, drive south on the Park Loop Road for about 6 miles, past the Cadillac Mountain entrance and the Bubble Pond parking lot, to the Bubble Rock parking on the right (west) side of the road. The trailhead departs from the Bubble Rock parking lot. GPS: N44 20.27' / W68 15.00'

The Hike

By going up into the gap between South and North Bubbles, this historic trail, dating back to the late 1800s, provides the shortest ascent to either of the rounded mountains that overlook Jordan Pond. The trip also goes to Bubble Rock a glacially deposited boulder known as an erratic, which sits atop South Bubble, and which generations of hikers have been photographed vainly trying to "push."

Heading west from the Bubble Rock parking lot, the trail crosses Jordan Pond Carry at 0.1 mile. At the junction with the northern section of the Bubbles Trail (formerly known as North Bubble Trail) at 0.3 mile, turn left (southwest) to head toward South Bubble and Bubble Rock.

At 0.4 mile, where Bubbles Divide continues straight ahead, turn left (southeast) to head toward South Bubble and Bubble Rock on the southern section of the Bubbles Trail (formerly known as the South Bubble Trail).

Follow the blue blazes and cairns along the trail and reach the 766-foot South Bubble summit at 0.6 mile. A sign points left (east) to nearby Bubble Rock, dumped here by glacier countless years ago from a spot more than 20 miles to the northeast, according to the National Park Service.

Close inspection of the 100-ton rock reveals large black and white crystals that are unlike the native pink granite Acadia, an indication that Bubble Rock came from afar. Generations ago, it was thought that floods of biblical proportions moved giant boulders around. But it was clues like Bubble Rock that led nineteenth-century scientist Louis Agassiz to theorize that massive glaciers once covered the earth.

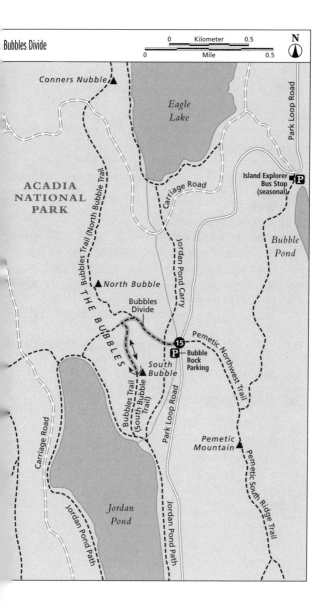

Bubbles Divide

Conners Nubble ▲

Eagle Lake

ACADIA NATIONAL PARK

Bubbles Trail (North Bubble Trail)

THE BUBBLES

▲ North Bubble

Bubbles Divide

Carriage Road

Jordan Pond Carry

Park Loop Road

Island Explorer Bus Stop (seasonal) P

Bubble Pond

Pemetic Northwest Trail

15 P Bubble Rock Parking

▲ South Bubble

Bubbles Trail (South Bubble Trail)

Carriage Road

Park Loop Road

Jordan Pond Path

Jordan Pond

Jordan Pond Path

Pemetic Mountain ▲

Pemetic South Ridge Trail

N

0   Kilometer   0.5
0   Mile   0.5

Return the way you came. Hardy hikers can make a 1.5-mile loop by heading steeply down the Bubbles Trail (South Bubble Trail) to the shores of Jordan Pond and turning sharply left (northeast) onto Jordan Pond Carry and then right (east) onto Bubbles Divide back to the parking lot.

Miles and Directions

0.0 Start at the Bubbles Divide trailhead, leaving from the Bubble Rock parking lot on the right (west) side of the Park Loop Road.

0.1 Cross the junction with Jordan Pond Carry.

0.3 Reach the junction with the northern section of the Bubbles Trail (formerly known as North Bubble Trail), and turn left (southwest) toward South Bubble and Bubble Rock.

0.4 At the junction where Bubbles Divide continues straight ahead, turn left (southeast) on the southern section of the Bubbles Trail (formerly known as South Bubble Trail), and head toward South Bubble and Bubble Rock.

0.6 Reach the South Bubble summit and Bubble Rock. Return the way you came.

1.2 Arrive back at the trailhead.

Mount Desert Island
West of Somes Sound

This is the quieter side of the island. The major "best easy" Acadia National Park trails on the west side of Mount Desert Island go up or around such landmarks as Acadia and Flying Mountains, Beech Mountain, Beech Cliff, and Ship Harbor.

The most popular routes in the western mountains of the park are the Acadia Mountain and Flying Mountain Trails, which offer close-up views of Somes Sound, the only fjord-like estuary on the East Coast of the United States; the trail to Beech Mountain to its fire tower; and the route to Beech Cliff, with its views down to Echo Lake.

The popular and easy trails to Ship Harbor, Wonderland, and Bass Harbor Head Light are near Bass Harbor. They go along the rocky pink-granite shore that makes Acadia stand out.

16 Acadia Mountain Trail

The hike to 681-foot Acadia Mountain is along one of the older trails in the park and leads to a beautiful outlook o Somes Sound, the only fjord-like feature on the Atlanti coast of the United States, and of nearby mountains such a Norumbega and Beech. Another good option is a short sid trip to Man o' War Brook, named for the French and Brit ish warships in the 1700s that came to get drinkable wate where the brook cascades into Somes Sound.

Distance: 2.8-mile lollipop
Hiking time: 1.5 to 2 hours
Difficulty: More challenging
Trail surface: Forest floor, rock ledges
Best season: Spring through fall, particularly early morning or late afternoon in summer to avoid the crowds
Other trail users: Horseback riders are allowed on the Man o' War Brook Trail section of the hike

Canine compatibility: Leashed dogs permitted but not recommended because of some steep sections
Nat Geo Trails Illustrated Topographic Map: Acadia National Park
Special considerations: Chemical toilet at parking lot across from the trailhead

Finding the trailhead: From Somesville head south on ME 102 for about 3 miles, past Ikes Point, to the Acadia Mountain parking lot on the right (west) side of ME 102. The trailhead is on the left (east) side of the road; be careful crossing the high-speed road. An Island Explorer bus stop is on the east side of ME 102, diagonally across from the Acadia Mountain parking lot. GPS: N44 19.18' / W68 19.5

popular trek on the west side of Somes Sound because
f its great views, the Acadia Mountain Trail also offers a
ouple of unusual features: It goes along the sole mountain
dge on Mount Desert Island that runs east to west instead
° north to south, and it takes you to a waterfall that tumbles
to Somes Sound.

Benjamin F. DeCosta, who explored more remote parts
° the island for his *Rambles in Mount Desert*, described
is trail in 1871, around the time the island first became
ite popular with hikers, according to *Pathmakers*, by the
ational Park Service's Olmsted Center for Landscape
eservation. Formerly called Robinson Mountain, Acadia
among many peaks in the park that were renamed under
orge B. Dorr's leadership as first park superintendent in
° early 1900s.

Severe erosion once hampered hikers on this trail, but
2016 the trails crew and the Friends of Acadia–supported
uth Conservation Corps completed a facelift on a section
t includes 135 new steps, repairs to other steps, and more
n 200 square feet of retaining wall.

The trail is easy at the start. From the trailhead across
n the parking lot, walk up sixteen steps, and turn imme-
ely left (north) onto a spur trail that parallels ME 102
takes you to the Island Explorer bus stop at 0.1 mile. At
bus stop head east into the woods and onto the gravel
1 o' War Brook Trail, an old fire road. At 0.2 mile turn
(northeast) to pick up the Acadia Mountain Trail, across
1 the junction with the Saint Sauveur Mountain Trail.
The trail continues its steady rise through cedar and pine,
1g you up a series of staircases of granite steps. Good

views of the sound are right ahead, and you may hear th sounds of boats.

To the west, Echo Lake, the fourth-largest lake in Acadia, comes into view behind you. The trail levels off a b and soon a couple of historic Bates-style cairns tip you off the peak. Here, from a rock promontory you get expansiv views of Somes Sound to the north and the Gulf of Main Sutton Island, and the rest of the Cranberry Isles to th south.

Somes Sound had long been considered the East Coas only fjord—a long, narrow, glacially carved ocean inlet and is still listed as such on some of the park informatio But in 1998 the Maine Geological Survey noted that it m be more properly described as a *fjard*, smaller than and not limited in water circulation as a true fjord.

Atop Acadia you may find turkey vultures soaring ov head, unmistakable with their massive size and small heads, or see and hear a peregrine falcon, as we have. T around here for a shorter out-and-back hike of 1.6 miles. continue on to complete the 2.8-mile lollipop.

If you choose to go on ahead, a tricky turn on the t directs you over jagged rock to a second peak of sorts at miles. This second broad, open summit provides a spler view—perhaps one of the best on the island. From Beech Mountain with its fire tower is to the west; Va Cove, Flying Mountain, and the Gulf of Maine are to south; and Somes Sound and Norumbega Mountain ar the east.

The trail descends steeply from this second peak, pro ing close-up views of the sound on the way down. At t it's handy to hold on to trees and rocks while headed d the rock face and crevices.

At 1.7 miles you reach a junction with a spur trail to Man o' War Brook Trail to the right (west) and a side trail to Man o' War Brook on the left (east), marked by a sign that says "Overlook." Turn left and follow stone steps to a nice spot near the base of a waterfall at 1.8 miles, with a view overlooking Somes Sound. When we were here in early June, the waterfall splashed along 20 to 30 feet of rock face and spilled into the sound. And during a visit in September, we saw a bald eagle fly by within 20 feet.

Return to the junction with the spur to the Man o' War Brook Trail, an old fire road, and go straight (west) on the spur trail to a major trail intersection with signs pointing to the old fire road and other points of interest. Bear right and take the old fire road northwest back to the junction with the Acadia Mountain Trail at 2.6 miles.

To return to the Island Explorer stop or the parking lot, continue straight on the Man o' War Brook Trail until it ends at the bus stop on ME 102 in another 0.1 mile. Turn left (south) onto the spur trail to return to the parking lot in another 0.1 mile.

Miles and Directions

0.0 Start from the trailhead across from the parking lot, and turn immediately left onto a spur trail paralleling ME 102 that takes you to the Island Explorer bus stop.

0.1 From the bus stop head east into the woods on the gravel Man o' War Brook Trail, an old fire road.

0.2 Pick up the Acadia Mountain Trail on the left (north) side of the gravel Man o' War Brook Trail, across from the junction with the Saint Sauveur Mountain Trail.

0.8 Reach the Acadia Mountain summit.

1.1 Reach a secondary summit.

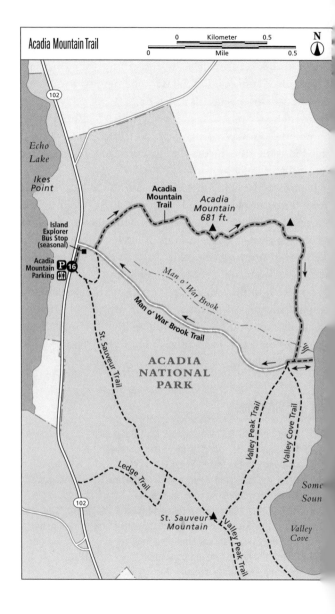

Acadia Mountain Trail

Kilometer
0   0.5
Mile
0   0.5

N

102

Echo
Lake

Ikes
Point

Acadia
Mountain
Trail

Acadia
Mountain
681 ft.

Island
Explorer
Bus Stop
(seasonal)

Acadia
Mountain
Parking   P 16

Man o' War Brook

Man o' War Brook Trail

ACADIA
NATIONAL
PARK

St. Sauveur Trail

Valley Peak Trail

Valley Cove Trail

Ledge Trail

102

St. Sauveur
Mountain

Valley Peak Trail

Some
Soun

Valley
Cove

1.7 At the junction with the spur to Man o' War Brook Trail and a side trail to Man o' War Brook, turn left (east) to an overlook.

1.8 Reach Man o' War Brook and Somes Sound overlook.

1.9 Return to the junction with the spur trail to Man o' War Brook Trail and head straight (west) to another major trail junction; bear right (northwest) to follow the old fire road.

2.6 Reach the junction with the Acadia Mountain Trail. Stay straight on the old fire road.

2.7 Reach the Island Explorer bus stop on ME 102. Turn left (south) onto the spur trail, paralleling ME 102.

2.8 Arrive back at the parking lot.

17 Flying Mountain Trail

This hike takes you up the lowest of twenty-six peaks i
Acadia, and yet it features one of the best panoramas, over
looking Somes Sound, Fernald Cove, and the Cranberr
Isles. There are views of Acadia and Norumbega Mountain
as well as excellent access to a large beach under the cliffs a
Valley Cove, where you might even see peregrine falcon
in flight.

Distance: 1.4-mile loop
Hiking time: About 1 hour
Difficulty: Moderate
Trail surface: Forest floor, rock ledges, gravel road
Best season: Spring through fall, particularly early morning and late afternoon in summer to avoid the crowds
Other trail users: Boaters and kayakers coming ashore in Valley Cove for day hikes, birders

Canine compatibility: Leashed dogs permitted but not recommended because of some steep sections
Nat Geo Trails Illustrated Topographic Map: Acadia National Park
Special considerations: No facilities

Finding the trailhead: From Somesville head south on ME 102 for about 4.5 miles, past the Saint Sauveur Mountain parking lot. Turn (east) onto Fernald Point Road and travel about 1 mile to the smal parking area at the foot of the gravel Valley Cove Trail, an old fire roa The trailhead is on the right (east) side of the parking area. The Isla Explorer bus does not stop here. GPS: N44 17.57' / W68 18.55'

's easy to see how Flying Mountain got its name, from the
ay the trail ascends swiftly to a bird's-eye view. In just 0.3
ile from the parking area, you reach the 284-foot summit
d its dramatic vistas.

The trail, first described in the late 1800s, climbs through
ep woods and then up rocky ledges. While in the shade of
e woods, hikers should be pleased that the National Park
rvice several years ago improved this old and well-trodden
il by adding log cribbing, or interlocked logs, to support
e steep climb. We counted ninety-three newer log steps
ght at the start of the ascent. The work helps prevent ero-
n and makes it an easier climb for children and others.
on granite ledges serve as stone steps, sometimes inter-
ersed with cribbing.

Once above tree line and at the top of the rock face, you
t views to the southeast of Greening Island and the Cran-
rry Isles. To the northwest are the rocky cliffs of Valley
ak. Dominating the view from the summit is the grassy
ninsula known as Fernald Point. Across the Narrows at
 mouth of Somes Sound is the town of Northeast Har-
r. From here you can look down on kayakers rounding
rnald Point or boaters entering and leaving Somes Sound.
u may even hear a ferry blow its whistle in Northeast
rbor, as we did on one of our climbs here. Somes Sound
50 feet deep in some spots but only 30 feet deep at the
rows.

Some hikers turn around here, content with the views
 Flying Mountain. But those who go on are rewarded
h scenes of Somes Sound; Valley Cove; and Norumbega,
dia, Penobscot, and Sargent Mountains. Some may even

be fortunate enough to see or hear peregrine falcons, which have returned to nesting in the cliffs above Valley Cove, one of Acadia's top conservation accomplishments.

"It's a feel-good story," said Bruce Connery, retired wildlife biologist at Acadia. "It is positive, positive, positive."

Peregrine falcons nearly became extinct in the 1960s but Rachel Carson's book *Silent Spring* alarmed the public and helped push the federal government to ban the pesticide DDT (which can dangerously thin eggshells) and pass the Endangered Species Act in 1972.

The park reintroduced peregrine falcons, and the first successful nest in thirty-five years occurred in 1991. Since then, more than 170 peregrine falcon chicks have fledged in the park, mainly at Valley Cove, Jordan Cliffs, and the precipice on the east face of Champlain Mountain. Acadia still runs an active banding program for the chicks.

The Flying Mountain Trail is noted for bird-watching, including for falcons, ospreys, and songbirds. On a recent hike, we took photos of a black-throated green warbler the woods just off the peak and spotted a falcon soaring high above.

Just beyond the summit of Flying Mountain, at 0.4 mile, you get the first glimpse of the northern reaches of Some Sound, as well as of Acadia Mountain to the north and Norumbega Mountain on the other side of the sound to the northeast. The ridge of Sargent and Penobscot Mountain just beyond that of Norumbega. There's a spur to an overlook to the right (east) before the trail begins its steep descent along large stone steps toward Valley Cove.

When the trail reaches the shore of the cove, go (west). A wooden bridge with a railing crosses a stream a separate hard-surface steps on each end converge at a she

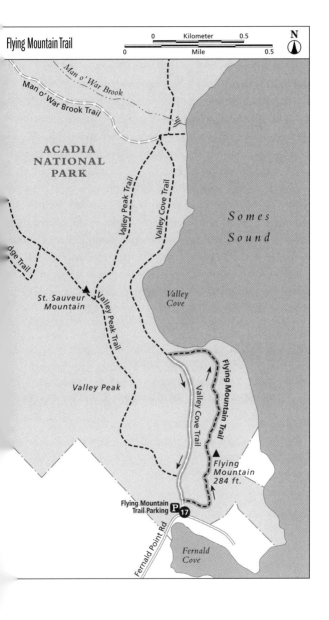

Kilometer
0   0.5

Mile
0   0.5

N

Man o' War Brook

Man o' War Brook Trail

ACADIA
NATIONAL
PARK

Valley Peak Trail

Valley Cove Trail

Somes
Sound

dge Trail

St. Sauveur
Mountain

Valley Peak Trail

Valley
Cove

Valley Peak

Valley Cove Trail

Flying Mountain Trail

Flying
Mountain
284 ft.

Flying Mountain
Trail Parking

P 17

Fernald Point Rd

Fernald
Cove

wide stairway that provides excellent access down to the rocky cove and pebble beach. There's lots of room, especially at low tide, and great views of steep, dark cliffs rising above the sound and of herring gulls soaring nearby.

The beach access was part of a rehabilitation in 2016 after the trail was damaged during the winter. In addition to two new wooden bridges, the work included more than 425 feet of new tread surface on the Flying Mountain Trail and new stone and log retaining walls.

At about 0.9 mile you reach the junction with the gravel Valley Cove Trail, an old fire road. Turn left (south) on the old fire road and loop back to the parking area at 1 miles. Hardy hikers can stay straight along the rocky shore of Valley Cove and add on a more challenging 1.0-mile section of the Valley Cove Trail that heads north, if it's not closed for peregrine falcon nesting season. A major upgrade of the Valley Cove Trail was finished in 2019.

Miles and Directions

0.0   Start at the Flying Mountain trailhead, on the east side of the parking area at the foot of the gravel Valley Cove Trail (an old fire road).

0.3   Reach the summit of Flying Mountain.

0.9   Turn left at the junction with Valley Cove Trail to loop back to the parking area.

1.4   Arrive back at the trailhead.

18 Beech Cliff Loop Trail

Enjoy cliff-top views of Echo Lake and beyond from this easy trail featuring a loop and out-and-back section. You can see the fire tower on nearby Beech Mountain from a rocky knob.

Distance: 0.7-mile lollipop
Hiking time: 30 minutes to 1 hour
Difficulty: Easy
Trail surface: Forest floor, graded gravel path, rock ledges
Best season: Spring through fall, particularly early morning or late afternoon in summer to avoid the crowds

Other trail users: Hikers going to the Canada Cliff Trail or coming up a difficult ladder climb from Echo Lake
Canine compatibility: Leashed dogs permitted
Nat Geo Trails Illustrated Topographic Map: Acadia National Park
Special considerations: Portable toilets at parking lot

Finding the trailhead: Head south from Somesville on ME 102 and turn right (west) at the flashing yellow light toward Pretty Marsh. Take the second left onto Beech Hill Road, at a sign pointing to Beech Mountain and Beech Cliff. Follow Beech Hill Road south for 3.2 miles to the parking lot at its end. The trailhead is across the parking lot, on the left (east) side of the road. The Island Explorer bus does not stop here, although there is a bus stop at Echo Lake, which is a difficult ladder climb away that is not recommended for the out of shape or faint of heart and is not allowed for dogs. GPS: N44 18.55' / W68 20.36'

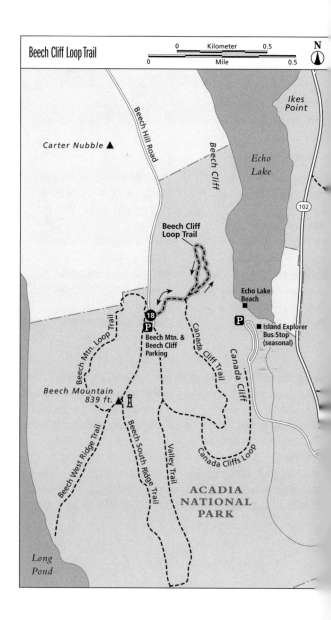

0   Kilometer   0.5

0   Mile   0.5

N

Ikes Point

Carter Nubble ▲

Beech Hill Road

Beech Cliff

Echo Lake

102

Beech Cliff Loop Trail

Echo Lake Beach

P

18

P

Beech Mtn. & Beech Cliff Parking

Beech Mtn. Loop Trail

Canada Cliff Trail

Island Explorer Bus Stop (seasonal)

Canada Cliff

Beech Mountain 839 ft.

Beech West Ridge Trail

Beech South Ridge Trail

Valley Trail

Canada Cliffs Loop

ACADIA NATIONAL PARK

Long Pond

The Hike

This is the easier of two ways to access Beech Cliff and its views because the trailhead is basically at the same elevation as the cliff. (The other way is a difficult ladder climb up Beech Cliff from Echo Lake.)

From the parking lot the trail rises gradually through the woods to a three-way junction at 0.2 mile, with the Canada Cliff Trail coming in on the right and Beech Cliff Loop ahead. Go straight (northeast) to head counterclockwise on the Beech Cliff Loop to access the views sooner, reaching Beech Cliff at 0.3 mile.

From Beech Cliff you can look down on Echo Lake Beach and the Appalachian Mountain Club (AMC) camp—but do not get too close to the edge. Acadia and Saint Sauveur Mountains are farther east. To the south are Somes Sound, the Gulf of Maine, and the Cranberry Isles; to the southwest is Beech Mountain, with its fire tower. You may also hear the traffic on ME 102, across the lake.

The trail continues along the cliff then circles inland, closing the loop at 0.5 mile back at the three-way junction. Bear right (west) to return to the parking lot at 0.7 mile.

Miles and Directions

0.0 Start at the Beech Cliff Loop trailhead, across the road (east) from the parking lot.

0.2 At the three-way junction with Canada Cliff Trail, go straight (northeast) to head counterclockwise on the Beech Cliff Loop and access the views sooner.

0.3 Reach Beech Cliff.

0.5 Circle back to close the loop at the junction with Canada Cliff Trail; bear right (west) back to the parking lot.

0.7 Arrive back at the trailhead.

19 Beech Mountain Loop Trail

This hike offers great views of Long Pond and Somes Sound along with a chance to climb to either the lower or the top platform of the park's only fire tower—a steel structure, still in good condition, atop 839-foot Beech Mountain. The trail is also a good place for bird-watching, including the migration of hawks; we saw four kestrels dive and soar above us during a hike one fall.

Distance: 1.1-mile loop
Hiking time: About 1 hour
Difficulty: Moderate
Trail surface: Forest floor, graded gravel path, rock ledges
Best season: Spring through fall
Other trail users: Hikers coming from the Beech South Ridge or Beech West Ridge Trail, birders

Canine compatibility: Leashed dogs permitted
Nat Geo Trails Illustrated Topographic Map: Acadia National Park
Special considerations: Portable toilets at parking lot

Finding the trailhead: Head south from Somesville on ME 102 and turn right (west) at the flashing yellow light toward Pretty Marsh. Take the second left onto Beech Hill Road, at a sign pointing to Beech Mountain and Beech Cliff. Follow Beech Hill Road south for 3.2 miles to the parking lot its end. The trailhead is at the northwest end of the parking lot. The Island Explorer bus does not stop here, although there is a stop at Echo Lake, a very steep climb away up a ladder trail. GPS: N44 18.54' / W68 20.37

The Hike

A must-hike in Acadia, Beech Mountain rises from a thin peninsula-like ridge of land sandwiched between Lo

Pond, the largest lake in Acadia at 897 acres, and Echo Lake, providing views all around. If you happen to hike Beech Mountain late one afternoon, you may be treated to a sunset that rivals the one you can get from Cadillac.

The trail begins off the parking lot and quickly leads to a loop at 0.1 mile.

The western half of this loop was carved in the 1960s as part of "Mission 66," an overhaul effort by the National Park Service to celebrate its fiftieth anniversary in 1966. The trail's eastern section is much older, appearing on a 1906 map, according to *Pathmakers*, a report by the NPS's Olmsted Center for Landscape Preservation.

Bear right (northwest) at the fork to head along the easier Mission 66 way (counterclockwise) around the loop up to the summit. You soon get spectacular views of Long Pond to the right (west) of the wide-open trail. At 0.6 mile you reach the junction with the Beech West Ridge Trail. Bear left (east). A series of log stairs leads to the summit.

At 0.7 mile you reach the steel fire tower atop Beech Mountain and the junction with the Beech South Ridge Trail. From the fire tower's first platform, which is always open, you can enjoy nearly 360-degree views of the ocean and surrounding mountains. Echo Lake, Acadia Mountain, and Saint Sauveur Mountain are to the east, while Southwest Harbor, Northeast Harbor, and the Cranberry Isles are to the southeast and Long Pond is to the west.

Gary Stellpflug, retired trails foreman at Acadia National Park, said the Beech Mountain fire tower is among a declining number of such towers that people can safely go up and down.

"It's a wonderful place," he said. "Everyone wants to go there. It's cool."

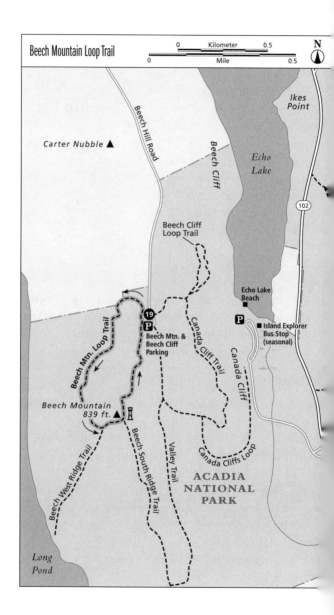

Beech Mountain Loop Trail

Kilometer
0   0.5

Mile
0   0.5

N

Beech Hill Road

Carter Nubble ▲

Beech Cliff

Ikes Point

Echo Lake

102

Beech Cliff Loop Trail

Echo Lake Beach

■ Island Explorer Bus Stop (seasonal)

19 P

Beech Mtn. & Beech Cliff Parking

Beech Mtn. Loop Trail

Canada Cliff Trail

P

Beech Mountain 839 ft. ▲

Canada Cliff

Beech West Ridge Trail

Beech South Ridge Trail

Valley Trail

Canada Cliffs Loop

ACADIA NATIONAL PARK

Long Pond

The Acadia trails crew has extensively rehabilitated the trail in recent years, adding log steps and drainage near the summit and completing similar work, with the help of the Acadia Youth Conservation Corps, on the west side of the loop in 2023.

According to the NPS, the fire tower was originally wooden, built around 1937 to 1941 by the Civilian Conservation Corps. It was replaced around 1960 to 1962 with a prefabricated steel tower flown in by helicopter and assembled on-site as part of the Mission 66 move to improve the parks. The NPS last staffed the tower, which is on the National Historic Lookout Register, in 1976.

From the summit bear left (north) at the junction with the Beech South Ridge Trail and loop back down quickly along the rough mountain face. Descend along switchbacks, open cliff face, and through boulder fields. Go down a series of stone steps and then log steps. Bear right (southeast) at a fork at 1.0 mile and return to the parking area at 1.1 miles.

Miles and Directions

- **0.0** Start at the Beech Mountain Loop trailhead, at the northwest corner of the parking lot.
- **0.1** Bear right (northwest) at the fork, going around the loop counterclockwise.
- **0.6** At the junction with the Beech West Ridge Trail, bear left (east) to circle up Beech Mountain.
- **0.7** Reach the Beech Mountain summit. Bear left (north) at the junction with the Beech South Ridge Trail to circle back down the mountain.
- **1.0** Bear right (southeast) at the fork.
- **1.1** Arrive back at the trailhead.

20 Wonderland

This very easy trail along an old road brings you to pink-granite outcrops along the shore and tide pools at low tide. You will see skunk cabbage, pitch pine, and wild sarsaparilla along the way and ponder why broken-up mussel shells are found inland along the trail rather than on the coastline.

Distance: 1.4 miles out and back
Hiking time: About 1 hour
Difficulty: Easy
Trail surface: Graded gravel road
Best season: Spring through fall, particularly early morning or late afternoon in summer to avoid the crowds; low tide for tidal pool exploration
Other trail users: Birders

Canine compatibility: Leashed dogs permitted
Nat Geo Trails Illustrated Topographic Map: Acadia National Park
Special considerations: Wheelchair accessible with assistance; closest facilities at Seawall picnic area or Ship Harbor Trail

Finding the trailhead: From Southwest Harbor head south about 1 mile on ME 102. Bear left (southeast) on ME 102A, passing the town of Manset in about 1 mile and Seawall Campground and picnic area in about 3 miles and reaching the Wonderland trailhead in about 4 miles. Parking is on the left (southeast) side of the road. The trail heads southeast along an abandoned gravel road toward the shore. The Island Explorer stops at Seawall Campground, a mile away, and passes by Wonderland on the way to Bass Harbor Campground. You may want to ask whether the bus driver will let you off at the Wonderland parking area. GPS: N44 14.01' / W68 19.12'

The Hike

Walk through the diverse forest, see the smooth pink granite along the shore and the birds, smell the salty sea, and explore the tide pools, and you will know why they call this Wonderland.

The easy trail along an old gravel road starts by winding through dark woods, but a huge smooth pink granite rock on the left soon hints at the show to come.

On the way to the shoreline, the trail goes by tall and feathery tamarack—a deciduous conifer that loses its needles in the fall—and then by wild sarsaparilla, which is thick in the ground cover, and cinnamon fern.

At about 0.1 mile go up a slight hill and make your way carefully among some roots and rocks. This is the toughest part of an otherwise gentle, well-graded trail.

During a "Birds and Botany of Wonderland" tour, Susan Hayward, a founder of the Maine Master Naturalist Program, pointed out flowers such as beach pea and black chokeberry, and woody plants like alder, shadbush, and a large mat of broom crowberry. She stopped next to some tall pitch pine, which is uncommon farther north of Acadia and has more needles per cluster and larger cones than jack pine, fairly common north and west of Acadia.

"Pitch pine is rare in this part of the woods," Hayward said. "It has a bundle of three needles per cluster," while jack pine has two.

Through the trees you begin to see the ocean on the right (southeast). At 0.7 mile the trail brings you to the shore, where the pink granite dramatically meets the sea. You can spend hours exploring here, especially when low tide exposes a bar to Long Ledge and tide pools with their

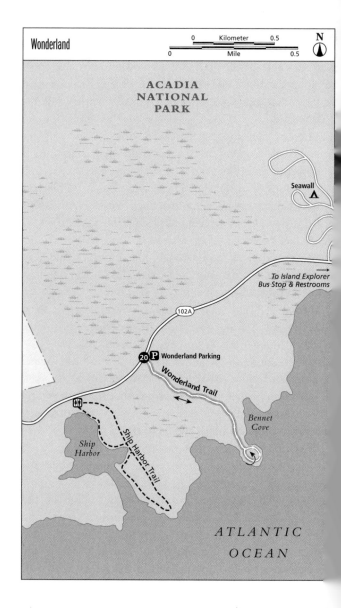

Wonderland

ACADIA
NATIONAL
PARK

Seawall

To Island Explorer
Bus Stop & Restrooms

102A

20 P Wonderland Parking

Wonderland Trail

Bennet
Cove

Ship
Harbor

Ship Harbor Trail

ATLANTIC
OCEAN

N

0   Kilometer   0.5
0   Mile   0.5

diverse marine life, from rockweed to barnacles to green crabs. Be careful of wet rocks, slick seaweed, and sudden waves.

Attending the annual Acadia Birding Festival, we were amazed to look through a scope and watch a flock of about three dozen black scoters diving headfirst into the ocean for food and then fluttering their wings upon emerging.

We also spotted an adult bald eagle, with its trademark white head and tail; a red-breasted nuthatch hopping on tree limbs; and songbirds such as a black-throated green warbler and a yellow-rumped warbler.

You can also take forever and a day to explore inland along the trail, as our nieces Sharon and Michelle did when we hiked this together, wondering about cracked-up sea-shells and seaweed found far from shore. We theorized that gulls must have dropped the mussel shells from midair to open them for food. That was proven later in the trip when we hiked the Bar Island Trail at low tide and witnessed that same gull-feeding activity. There are many things to wonder about along Wonderland.

Return the way you came.

Miles and Directions

0.0 Start at the Wonderland trailhead, on the southeast side of ME 102A, at the edge of the parking area.
0.1 The trail heads slightly uphill.
0.7 Reach the shoreline, where you can add on a loop to explore the rocky outcroppings. Return the way you came.
1.4 Arrive back at the trailhead.

21 Ship Harbor Trail

With a maritime mystery in its past, a huge undeveloped harbor, and sprawling pink granite, the Ship Harbor Trail epitomizes a lot about hiking the coast of Acadia National Park. President Barack Obama chose the trail as one of only a few he hiked with his wife and daughters during a visit in July 2010.

Distance: 1.3-mile figure-eight loop

Hiking time: About 1 hour

Difficulty: Easy

Trail surface: Graded gravel path, forest floor, rocky shore, log bridges

Best season: Spring through fall, particularly early morning or late afternoon in summer to avoid the crowds; low tide to explore tidal pools

Other trail users: Visitors with wheelchairs or baby strollers

Canine compatibility: Leashed dogs permitted

Nat Geo Trails Illustrated Topographic Map: Acadia National Park

Special considerations: The first 0.25 mile of the trail is on a hard-packed surface, making it accessible to visitors with wheelchairs or baby strollers. There is chemical toilet at the trailhead.

Finding the trailhead: From Southwest Harbor head south about 1 mile on ME 102. Bear left (southeast) on ME 102A, passing the town of Manset in about 1 mile, Seawall Campground and picnic area in about 3 miles, and the Wonderland Trail parking area in about 4 miles. The Ship Harbor trailhead is about 0.2 mile beyond Wonderland. The trailhead parking lot is on the left (south) side of ME 102A. The Island Explorer stops at Seawall Campground, more than a mile away, and passes by Ship Harbor Trail on the way to Bass Harbor Campground.

You may want to ask whether the bus driver will let you off at the Ship Harbor Trail parking area. GPS: N44 13.54' / W68 19.31'

The Hike

The trail is one of the easiest and most popular in Acadia, maybe because it offers so much: a thick spruce forest, wildflowers and lowbush blueberries in season, expanses of flat granite for relaxing next to the surf, intimate views of the islands, and the drama of the sea crashing against immense cliffs.

Located on the southern shore of the west side of Mount Desert Island, the hike is composed of two loops, or a figure eight, totaling 1.3 miles, with colorful new wayside exhibits that explain sea life in the flats and tide pools.

The history of Ship Harbor and the trail is also fascinating. The name of the harbor may stretch back to the fall of 1739, when some believe it was the site of the wreck of the *Grand Design*, an English vessel carrying Irish immigrants to Pennsylvania. A park-wide archaeological study in 2004 found evidence that suggests the name of the harbor may stem from that disaster, though there is no definitive proof.

The trail itself took decades to reach fruition. Park pioneers George B. Dorr and John D. Rockefeller Jr. worked to provide roadside access to Ship Harbor as early as the 1930s, and it was queued up to be completed by the Civilian Conservation Corps, but the work was left undone when the Corps disbanded in the park at the onset of World War II. It was finally completed in 1957 as part of a national program to improve the National Park System in time for its fiftieth anniversary in 1966.

Important new work was finished in 2015, when the entire first, or inner, 0.6-mile loop was improved and regraded to comply with access standards for those with physical disabilities, according to Gary Stellpflug, retired Acadia trails foreman.

During the hike, when you reach the first fork, at 0.1 mile at the base of the figure-eight loop, bear right (south) following the hard-packed surface to the edge of the Ship Harbor channel and the mudflats, which can be viewed at low tide. The trail now begins to get rocky and uneven as it approaches an intersection at 0.3 mile, in the middle of the figure-eight loop. Bear right along the graded surface to the edge of the Ship Harbor channel.

At low tide, the mudflats on the channel are ideal for exploring.

Common eiders are often seen floating at the mouth of Ship Harbor, and it's possible to catch glimpses along the trail of a bald eagle or osprey or even of such uncommon birds as a palm warbler or an olive-sided flycatcher. At 0. mile, near the mouth of Ship Harbor, you reach the rock shore along the Atlantic. Here you can admire the dramatic pink cliffs or explore tidal pools at low tide, when barnacle rockweed, snails, and other sea life are exposed by the receding waters. Granite cliffs stretch to the edge of the ocean shore at the tip of this loop.

Turn left to circle back along the remaining section of the figure-eight loop. When you reach an intersection at 1 mile, back at the center of the figure-eight loop, bear right (northwest) to continue along the hilly inland section of the loop, which is now well graded and accessible. Or, if you are tempted to return along the Ship Harbor channel, you

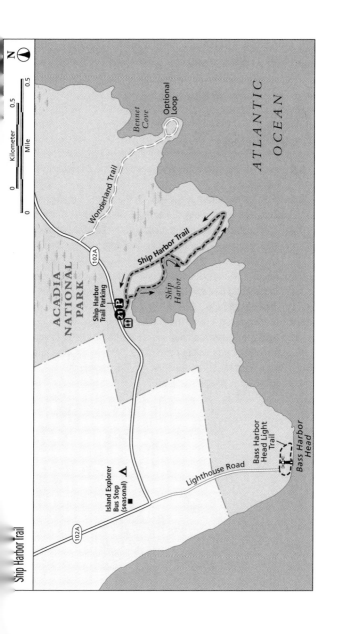

Ship Harbor Trail

can bear left at this intersection instead to retrace your steps along the channel northwest back to the trailhead.

At a fork at the base of the figure–eight loop, bear northwest for 0.1 mile to return to the parking lot.

Miles and Directions

0.0 Start at the Ship Harbor trailhead, on the left (south) side of ME 102A.

0.1 Bear right (south) at the fork, at the base of the figure-eight loop, and head along the edge of the Ship Harbor channel.

0.3 At the intersection in the middle of the figure-eight loop, bear right again to continue along the edge of the Ship Harbor channel.

0.7 Reach the rocky shoreline along the Atlantic and turn left (northwest) to circle back along the hilly inland section of the figure-eight loop.

1.0 At the intersection in the middle of the figure-eight loop, bear right (northwest) to continue along the hilly inland section.

1.2 Reach the fork at the base of the figure-eight loop and bear right (northwest) to head back to the parking lot.

1.3 Arrive back at the trailhead.

22 Bass Harbor Head Light Trail

Get a close-up view of the only lighthouse on Mount Desert Island, which uses a 1,000-watt red beacon to guide lobster boats and other mariners safely over the shoals to Bass Harbor. On one side of the parking lot, stairs bring you down the steep bluff to an overlook that provides views not only of Bass Harbor Head Light but also of Blue Hill Bay and Swans Island. On the other side, follow a paved path to stand under the lighthouse and read displays about its history.

Distance: 0.4 mile out and back

Hiking time: About 30 minutes

Difficulty: Moderate

Trail surface: Wooden deck and stairs, graded gravel path, rock ledges and steps, paved walkway

Best season: Spring through fall, particularly early morning or late afternoon in summer to avoid the crowds

Other trail users: None

Canine compatibility: Leashed dogs permitted

Nat Geo Trails Illustrated Topographic Map: Acadia National Park

Special considerations: There is a chemical toilet at the edge of the parking lot near the trailhead. The automated lighthouse is not open to the public; neither is the former lighthouse keeper's house. Hike the trail only in safe conditions—that is, not when it's stormy or when surf is crashing against the cliffs.

Finding the trailhead: From Bass Harbor head south about 0.6 mile on ME 102A until you reach a sharp curve in the road, where ME 102A heads left (east). Go straight ahead (south) on the 0.5-mile dead-end Lighthouse Road that takes you to the Bass Harbor Head Light parking. The trail begins on the left (southeastern) edge of the parking lot, across from the toilets. The Island Explorer bus does not stop here, though there is a Bass Harbor Campground stop near the beginning of the dead-end road to the lighthouse. GPS: N44 13.21' / W68 20.13'

The Hike

Maine is synonymous not only with lobster but also with lighthouses.

More than sixty towering beacons still stand guard along the state's 3,500 miles of rocky coastline, with perhaps one of the most photogenic being Bass Harbor Head Light in Acadia National Park. Certainly the contrast of Acadia's distinctive pink granite against the lighthouse's white tower makes for a picture-postcard view, and many visitors come to create a picture of their own.

Built in 1858, the lighthouse, originally lit with a brass lamp fired by whale oil, even today directs boaters safely in and out of Bass Harbor and Blue Hill Bay with its red beacon that was automated in 1974.

The National Park Service, which owns lighthouses on Bear Island and Baker Island in the park, also agreed in 202 to accept ownership of Bass Harbor Head Light from the US Coast Guard and maintain it in accord with federal standards for historic properties. The park has been considering possible uses and also ways to manage traffic at the popular lighthouse. Parking is often tight, with only about twenty-five spaces in the lot; parking is not permitted along the road to the lighthouse or along Route 102A.

Parking is so sparse at the light station—the No. 5 destination in the entire park—that the NPS warns people expect traffic "gridlock at sunset," the most popular time visit. Because of the significant crowding issues, open space at the light station may exist during the day only, well before sunset. The NPS also asks that visitors respect neighbors and private property owners.

From the parking lot the trail splits into two 0.2-mile sections on either side of the light station; each offers revealing views and different experiences.

On the southeastern edge of the parking lot across from the toilets, head southeast along the trail through the woods to a wooden staircase. Volunteers do an amazing amount of work behind the scenes at Acadia, and this staircase is another example; two volunteers, Mark Munsell and Jerry Hopcroft, did almost all of the carpentry in rebuilding the stairs in 2019. The project included new secure handrails, thirty-three new wooden steps, and three new viewing or rest platforms on the stairway.

Go down the steep stairs and loop back along the rocks toward the lighthouse to an overlook. The length of this section of trail, only 0.1 mile one way to the overlook, makes it seem easy, but its steepness, even on wooden stairs, makes it moderately difficult. Take your time. Let the stunning views take your breath away, not overexertion.

From the overlook the view includes Bass Harbor Head Light, the ocean, and outlying islands, including Swans Island, which has a year-round population serviced by a vehicle ferry from Bass Harbor.

If you clamber along the rocks to get different perspectives, be careful. The rocks can be slippery, especially when wet.

Return the way you came and then cross the parking lot to pick up the trail on the other side of the lighthouse.

The trail on the southwestern edge of the lot allows visitors to stand under the 32-foot-high lighthouse, touch the white-brick exterior, and view two shipshape bells while enjoying scenic views of the ocean and the craggy cliffs below.

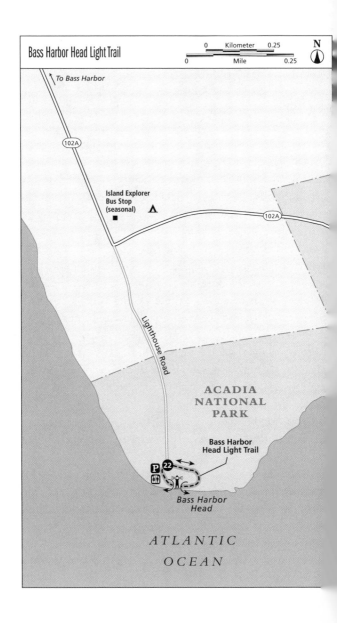

Bass Harbor Head Light Trail

0   Kilometer   0.25
0   Mile   0.25

N

To Bass Harbor

102A

Island Explorer
Bus Stop
(seasonal)   ▲
■

102A

Lighthouse Road

ACADIA
NATIONAL
PARK

Bass Harbor
Head Light Trail

P 22

Bass Harbor
Head

ATLANTIC
OCEAN

Along the 0.1-mile paved path are some enlightening educational exhibits. Stop and read displays about key dates in the history of the light station, details of its ten-sided lantern, and the proper care of a fog bell and other recurring and demanding duties of a lighthouse keeper.

Bass Harbor Head Light can be jam-packed, especially on a nice summer weekend close to sunset. But former president Barack Obama toured it during his vacation at the park in July 2010, and maybe you should too.

Return the way you came.

Miles and Directions

0.0 Start at the Bass Harbor Head Light trailhead, on the left (southeastern) edge of the parking lot.

0.1 Reach the overlook at the end of the wooden stairs and rock path, with views of Bass Harbor Head Light, Blue Hill Bay, and outlying islands. Return the way you came.

0.2 Arrive back at the parking lot and cross to pick up a paved path on the northwestern edge of the lot.

0.3 Reach the western side of the lighthouse. Retrace your steps.

0.4 Arrive back at the trailhead.

Hike Index